A Guide to Oriental Rugs

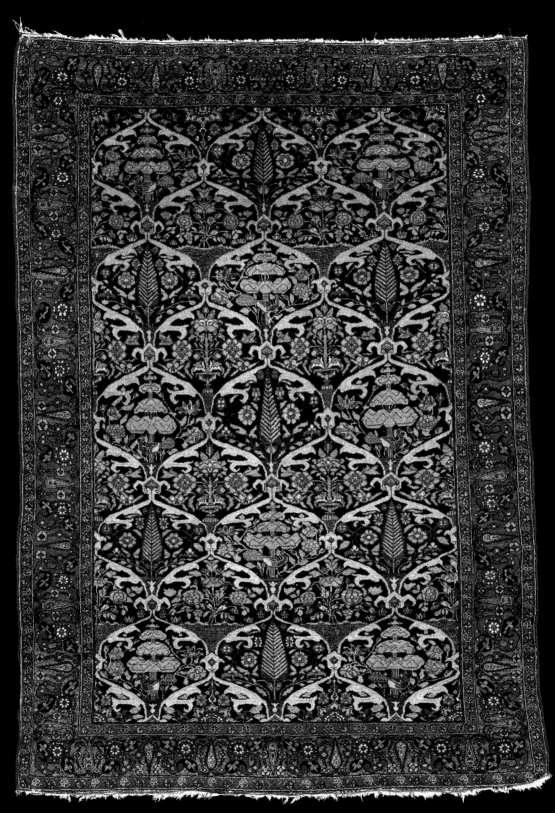

Bakhtiar pile rug, 1.9 × 1.35 m. One of a pair of rugs made in the Chahar Mahal district of Iran during the late 19th century. John Leach Tribal Rug and Kilim Gallery

A Guide to
Oriental Rugs

Peter Winch

Kangaroo Press

Front cover: Main picture—Tabriz pile rug, 3.8 × 2.8 m. Late 19th century. *Nomadic Rug Traders.* Insert—Senneh kilim, 1.5 × 1.45 m, 19th century. *Nomadic Rug Traders.*
Back cover: Carpet repair stall in Peshawar, Pakistan, 1984.

First published in 1991 by Kangaroo Press Pty Ltd
3 Whitehall Road (P.O. Box 75) Kenthurst NSW 2156
Typeset by G.T. Setters Pty Limited
Printed in Hong Kong by Colorcraft Ltd

ISBN 0 86417 373 X

Contents

Acknowledgments

As well as thanking my ever patient wife and children who have encouraged my interest in oriental rugs and travel to source countries for more than ten years, I would like to thank Leigh and Alexandra Copeland, Ross and Irene Langlands, John Leach, Tony Whiting, Bill Evans, Ian Humphries and Jalal Ali Gorgi for their individual inputs into my understanding of the oriental rug market and appreciation of ethnographic weavings.

Another professional group whose long term input to my work has helped make this book possible are the editors of those newspapers and magazines who have helped support my interest in rugs and travel and made it possible for me to share my experiences with their readers. Special thanks must go to Tony Berry, Julie and Alan Carter, Barry Cooke, Annie Cochrane, Alexander MacRobbie and the features editors of the *Newcastle Herald*, most recently, Roger Brock.

Special thanks also to Ross and Irene Langlands and John Leach for their efforts in editing portions of this text for technical information, and to Rajab and Ali in Pakistan.

Some photographs from this book have been previously published in *Signature, Australasian Post, The Sun, AustralAsian Holiday, Living With Antiques* and *The Antique Trader* and Chapter 11 is taken from an article which was published in *The Antique Trader*.

Photography

Peter Winch—Photographs on pages 11, 12, 13, 17 (top left and right), 19, 20, 25 (left), 27, 28, 30 (left top and bottom), 33, 34, 37, 40, 41 (right), 43, 46 (left cente and bottom right), 47, 48, 53 (right), 56 (top), 58 (right centre and bottom), 64 (left), 66 (left), 67, 77 (left), 87 and 91 (top and centre), © Peter Winch, June 1990.

Grant Hancock—Photographs on pages 8, 22, 25 (right), 26, 59, 60, 68, 69, 72.

Nigel Brockhoff—Photographs on pages 17 (bottom left), 30 (right top and bottom), 41 (left), 46 (top), 53 (left), 58 (top), 66 (top and right).

Alan Schultz—Photograph on page 91 (bottom).

Photographs on cover and pages 50, 54, 57, 62, 63, 78, 81, 82, 84, 88 and 89 supplied by Nomadic Rug Traders, Harris St, Pyrmont, NSW.

Photographs on pages 26, 55, 73, 74, 77 (right), 80 and 83 supplied by R. & G. Lindley.

Photographs on pages 2, 36, 64 (right) and 76 supplied by John Leach Tribal Rug and Kilim Gallery, Rathdowne St, North Carlton, Victoria.

Line drawings All line drawings and map by Ben Winch © Ben Winch, June 1990.

Introduction

Many people have difficulty making an informed decision about the type of oriental rug which most suits their needs. The popular marketing hypes, large scale discounting of commercial products, modern day sales myths and slogans and the huge array of carpets to be found only help to confuse the ill informed and I decided that a 'guide book' to the hand made rugs which are presently on the market would help an inexperienced person to make more rational decisions when assessing the products offered.

I have tried to arrange the information in a way that makes comparative judgements between rugs of a similar production background possible as well as describing the identifying features of major rug types. It must however be remembered that no black and white rules can be applied to any type of oriental rug, as when an all encompassing generalisation on a specific rug type is made, inevitably a rug is discovered that doesn't conform to the rule. This is what makes an oriental rug a uniquely individual item.

This book was written to be a guide to classification and assessment of groups of oriental rugs and to help those who have just begun to appreciate this unique artform to understand the background of carpets produced at different times, by different ethnic groups and in different countries of the world. I hope that the selection of carpets that I have included in the book will also be of interest to readers who have a good knowledge of the subject as I believe that no-one else has grouped this particular range of weaving styles or production sources into one book in recent times.

In a work of this size it is impossible to cover all the rug weaving centres and tribal groups who created hand knotted carpets, but I have included a range of the major rug types which can be found in retail outlets, auction catalogues and source centres at the time of writing. I have also tried not to use too much rug jargon to describe design motifs and rug details but to present the information in an easy to understand way and in everyday language.

It should also be noted that the spelling of the names of tribal groups, towns or generic labels for household goods is my personal choice and that other authors have chosen different words. Most of the terms originate outside the English language and the question of spelling seems a matter of phonetics so I have tried to use spelling which conveys the sound of the word as much as possible.

I hope that after reading this book you will have an understanding of the varieties of hand made rugs that can be found as well as a basis for assessing examples. When interpreting the information it must always be remembered that oriental rugs are individual items and that personal preferences regarding design motifs, colours, use and reasons for purchase must be of overriding concern. The information in this book is only a guide to identification of carpet types and a method of assessing the individual merit and uses of specific items.

Old Saltuq pile rug, 2.9 X 2.1 m. Early 20th century from the north of Afghanistan. Author's collection

1 What is an Oriental Rug?

The term oriental rug refers to a hand woven or hand knotted floor covering that has been produced on a loom. The sizes, designs, colours and materials used are diverse and a wide variety of carpets and kilims have been and are still produced. The oldest known hand knotted rug was discovered in a frozen tomb in Russia and has been dated around the fifth century. Researchers believe that rugs have been hand knotted since this time in the Central Asian region and that they were probably produced within a tribal environment.

There are sixteenth century pieces in museums and it is known that the courts of various Persian and Ottoman emperors encouraged weaving and supported groups of the finest weavers. The Persian empire carried weaving skills to India and the Ottomans influenced carpet making in Turkey as well as the cultural environment of Central Asia.

By the late nineteenth century oriental rugs were being made in and exported from various regions of what are now known as Morocco, Roumania, Turkey, Iran, Afghanistan, the Caucasus Mountains and Trans-Caspian States of the USSR, Pakistan, India and China.

One hundred years later, in response to increasing demands from Western markets, these areas have been affected by a mass commercialisation of production with many workshops and factories creating rugs. Other countries have also tried to enter the market place and carpets have been, and in some cases still are being made in Yugoslavia, Bulgaria, Bangladesh, Nepal, Thailand and Hong Kong.

To make an oriental rug the threads used for the base weave, called the *warp* threads, are strung on a loom which is usually made out of wood. Most looms used in modern times stand vertically to the ground and are called *vertical looms*. This type of loom has been used in many countries over a long period of time but its use is confined to situations where it is not likely to be moved, i.e. in the home or a community workshop. The advantages of this type of loom

are that the tension of the weaving is kept fairly constant as the wooden frame is quite rigid, the loom is usually well constructed, often having been made for the specific environment where it is to be used, and the rugs produced are therefore more likely to have a rectangular shape.

In nomadic or very primitive environments, looms are made out of the trunks of small trees which are staked to the ground for tensioning and the heddle, which separates every alternative warp thread to enable the weaving process, is made from thinner branches, tied to the individual warps and attached to a primitive frame work. This type of loom is called a *horizontal loom*. The products from a horizontal loom are less likely to be perfectly symmetrical and often have sides which are not parallel. This misshapen appearance is also caused by the loom being dismantled during the weaving process when nomads have to follow their flocks with the seasons, moving to high altitudes in the summer and down to the plains again in winter.

No matter what type of loom is used, the process of producing a hand knotted rug is the same. To begin the rug a few rows of *weft* threads are passed through the warps which are strung on the loom. This gives a base to begin making the carpet. Wool of different colours is then tied to pairs of warp threads to create a pattern. This process is continued across the width of the warps then some weft threads, sometimes up to three or four, are passed between the warps.

Every alternate warp is covered by the first weft, then the heddle lifts the threads that were depressed and another is passed through the weaving so that the opposite warps are covered. After the wefts are inserted the weaver beats them down the warps with a metal comb to tension the weaving.

Once the desired tension is obtained another row of knots is tied then more wefts inserted and the process is repeated until the entire loom is covered with hand tied pile. The different coloured knots create the pattern of the carpet and, as the pile is an integral part of the weaving the pattern can be seen on the back as well as the front of the rug. After the rug is completed the warp ends are cut and consolidated, often just by being knotted together in clumps of six or so. In some types of rugs the warp ends are intricately braided, others show three or more rows of macrame type knotting before the warp ends are free.

These loose warp ends are what form the fringe of an oriental carpet and individual production centres or sources treat the loose warps in different ways, helping a student of rugs to identify particular items.

The final process in the production of the rug is to trim the pile to an even height, the overstitching, if necessary, of the sides of the rug—these are called the selvedges and in some cases are bound when the rug is on the loom and do not require attention afterwards—then the carpet is usually washed.

Two major types of knot are used to tie the pile to the warps, the Senneh or asymmetrical knot and the Ghiordes or symmetrical knot.

The value or durability of a rug is not dependent on which type of knot was used to make it, but recognising which knot was used in a particular piece can aid the identification of the geographic area in which it was made, the tribe who created it or the environment in which it was produced. There are some other methods which are used to knot rugs, the most common found in Nepal and India where Tibetan refugees loop the wool around a thin metal rod at the same time as tying it to the warps and the pile is created by cutting the thread along the rod, turning the many loops of wool into tufts of pile.

In most cases, rugs which utilise a symmetrical knot have fewer knots per square inch than those which have been made with an asymmetrical knot, but this is not always the case and it must be noted that the amount of knots of pile in a square inch is not an overriding concern when trying to assess the value or durability of a particular carpet.

Another large group of weavings which are described as oriental rugs are known collectively as *kilims*. These rugs are flatwoven by a variety of methods and do not usually have any piled work, although some mixed technique weavings, often old household items from primitive environments, utilised many types of flatweave and had hand knotted highlights.

A common method used in weaving kilims is the *slitwoven tapestry* technique. The warps are strung on the loom but no pile knots are tied. Instead dyed weft threads are used to create the pattern, woven under and over alternate warps until the design demands a different colour. At this point another weft is begun and the different coloured area woven, but the closest the colours get is adjacent warp threads and there remains a small gap in the rug where the design colours meet.

This method inhibits designs which contain longitudinal lines which would create long slits along the warp threads of the rug. Most are stepped patterns where very small ledges are formed along the edges of diamond type shapes so that only very small slits appear. Many early Turkish kilims utilising this weaving style must have been extremely difficult to make as the weaving is very fine and the steps of the design very intricate in order to overcome this structural disadvantage.

Symmetrical knot (Ghiordes)

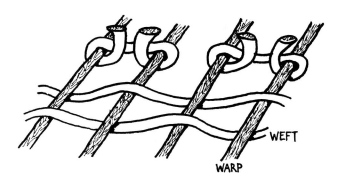

Asymmetrical knot (Senneh)

Slitwoven tapestry

A way of solving the problem of small gaps in the kilim is to use the *double interlocking* tapestry method of weaving. In this instance the weaving style is the same as the slitwoven method except where two colours meet. The weft threads share a warp, enabling sharper pattern points and designs with straight lines which run along the warp threads to be made and creating a more solid surface.

Double interlocking tapestry

Intricate patterns can be obtained when the *floating weft brocade* technique is used. The weft threads appear on the front of the kilim when they are necessary to the pattern, usually only being woven through small numbers of warps, then they 'float' on the back of the rug as the next colour is woven with the warps and appears in the pattern on the front. Floating weft kilims often have patterns consisting of stripes from 2 to 20 cm wide which are filled with finely detailed motifs and alternate with an equivalent width of plain weave. Some very finely woven examples are covered with weft brocade and are quite thick as the weft threads are two or three deep in the rug when they 'float' on the back. The main disadvantage of this type of kilim is that the pattern can only be seen from the front whereas a slit woven or double interlocking tapestry can be used on either side.

Floating weft brocade (front)

Floating weft brocade (back)

Fine design details are also achieved by a method of *weft wrapping* where the coloured weft threads always cover two warps then are looped behind one of these before covering the next two. The pattern is created by weaving small areas with different colours and the loose weft ends are left hanging long at the back of the rug when the area of colour is completed. This method allows for very intricate detail as well as producing a very durable rug as the loose wefts create a thick backing for the piece. It is commonly called Soumak, probably after a town in the Caucasus Mountains of what is now the USSR where kilims in this style were made, but the name does not imply any specific geographical region when used in this context.

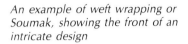

An example of weft wrapping or Soumak, showing the front of an intricate design

The same piece of weft wrapping or Soumak showing the back

The other major forms of adornments used in kilims are types of *extra weft* brocades where a plainweave item is decorated by the addition of extra, coloured wefts. Through a study of different examples I have assumed that some of these designs are added after the weaving is completed and are therefore a type of embroidery. The Cicim (local pronunciation sounded like Djidjim) style of rugs which I found when buying in Turkey during the mid-eighties seemed to fit into this category but other items I have seen, especially those coming from the north-west of Iran and the Caucasus Mountains, appear to have had the coloured pattern woven at the same time as the base weave.

Extra weft brocade or Cicim

2 Spinning and Dyeing

Before a carpet or kilim can be made the threads used in the production must be obtained and those needed for decoration of the piece must be dyed in the appropriate colours for the pattern. Once a fleece is obtained the wool needs to be carded, spun and plied, using, at the most primitive level, a rock or small piece of stick, a drop spindle, hand spinning wheel or modern, automated spinning and plying machine. The spun thread can be plied by hand and in a primitive environment this can be done by tying a rock to one end of two or more spun threads then swinging it around the head in ever increasing arcs as the yarns are slowly twisted together.

A structural detail that is often included in the technical analysis of a rug is the direction in which the wool fibres were spun and plied. When the twist of the yarn is counter clockwise it is known as Z spun, which means that the fibre was spun by twisting it to the right. In S spun yarns the fibre was spun to the left and when viewed shows a twist in a clockwise direction. It is usual for spun thread to be plied in the opposite way to the direction of spin.

The wool for the base weave is often left undyed but the pile material needs to be coloured in order to produce a pattern. Historically, this process was performed either by a master dyer who learned his trade as a child and knew the recipes for different colours and colour tones which could be produced from vegetable material found growing close to the village or along a tribe's migratory route, or, in some cases, by the family group who produced the weaving.

Dyeing was often done in small batches and it is common to find different shades of the same or a very similar colour throughout a single rug. These different tones often occur in defined segments of the rug and appear as stripes of colour. This effect is known as Abrash and should not be thought of as detracting from the rug.

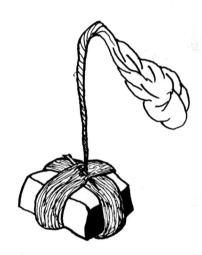

Primitive spinning tool made from a rock

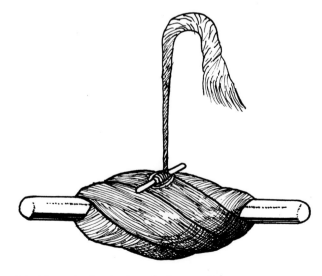

Primitive spinning tool made from a stick

A wooden drop spindle

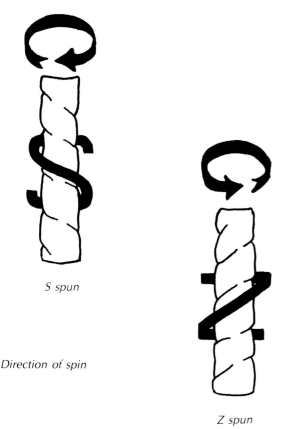

S spun

Direction of spin

Z spun

The wool fibre, when observed through a microscope, shows small scales covering the entire surface (these scales are one of the reasons that the wool fibre is so durable). To dye the wool it is necessary to immerse it in a mordant solution which causes these scales to open. then it is placed in the dye and the colour can impregnate the fibre without damaging the protective scales. Traditionally some colours were very difficult to produce without damaging the wool fibres as only vegetable products were available. A black colour almost always required a dye stuff or mordant containing an ingredient which caused the dyed wool to slowly oxidise.

Many antique tribal and village pieces can be found in excellent condition except for the dark brown or black areas of the pile. These portions of the design have oxidised, often down to the base weave, and the rug shows indentations in the pile where this has occurred. This effect can be seen, to a lesser degree, in many rugs which use the dyestuff madder to obtain a variety of red tones. The mordant used to produce brighter shades also had a corrosive effect.

The first chemical dyes were known as aniline dyes and appeared in rug producing areas around the 1870s. There were many problems with these dyes and it was found that most were not fast, fading either when exposed to water or to light. Not all rug weavers used these dyes and, in fact, few rugs survive in which they can be found.

The twentieth century saw a large range of man-made dyes but, in many remote areas, primitive dyestuffs, of both vegetable and chemical origin, are still used. Modern dyeing techniques and chrome type dyes can produce a huge range of colours which usually do not fade and have little if any detrimental effect on the wool fibre.

These are used in most large production environments and the main danger to modern day buyers is carpets which have been chemically treated after production in order to make the pile more lustrous or to give the carpet an aged appearance. The rug is washed in a harsh solution, which can be of strong acid or alkaline content. This strips the wool fibres of their protective scales and enables them to reflect more light and look more lustrous. Unfortunately, this process severely damages the fibres and a rug which has been treated in this manner will have a greatly diminished lifespan: I have seen some carpets treated in this way that have begun to shed large patches of pile after only six years of use.

Usually the treatment for artificially ageing a rug does not damage it as severely but the wool fibres are still weakened and the pile tends to have a dull and lifeless look. In this instance the carpet is washed in a bleach, like a lime solution, to fade the colours or left in the street to be used by a large bulk of people and faded by the sun. It seems a grossly inadequate way of imitating age as antique, vegetable dyed carpets usually show bright and intense colours even after years of use.

Tibetan woman carding wool in preparation for hand spinning, Nepal, 1989

Vat dying wool in Nepal, 1989

Corrosion of the dark coloured ground can be seen in this old Baluch rug. Author's collection

3 Categories of Oriental Rugs

Once you know what an oriental rug is it is useful to categorise examples so that their individual merit can be measured against examples from a similar source. It would be pointless to try and assess a carpet from a primitive source with the same yardstick used to evaluate a workshop produced item.

A common classification system is to divide rugs into groups depending on the environment in which they were produced. The four major groups are the court carpets, which are only available to the very wealthy collector or museum, workshop produced rugs, village rugs and tribal rugs. Once an understanding of these categories is reached it is possible to look at both the modern production and old or antique rugs in a more defined and structured context.

Court Carpets

These very rare carpets were made in the courts of various Persian and Ottoman emperors. They were usually very finely knotted, often including spun gold thread in flat-woven patches. Very large carpets in curvilinear designs of flowers, gardens or hunting scenes were produced and nearly all surviving examples are housed in museums.

Workshop Carpets

Workshops began when the demand for oriental rugs, especially in the West, created a need for greater and more organised production. Large dealers chose designs especially for their customers' homes and decorating requirements.

The most popular sizes were made and traditional colours were blended with the new fashion tones demanded by the export market. Some of the most famous and valuable workshop rugs came from the Mahal, Heriz and Tabriz areas of northwest Iran and were designed by important interior decorators of the late nineteenth century.

In workshops the design of a rug is drawn onto a piece of graph paper and the intersection points of the graph lines are organised in such a way that they represent a single knot of pile, i.e. each vertical line is a warp thread and at the intersection of the horizontal line a knot will be tied which covers two warp threads. Artists make 'cartoons', as these sheets are called, and workers sit at looms, often three or four to a carpet, knotting the design to the base and using the graph paper as a map.

In many modern workshops the wool for the pile is purchased pre-spun and dyed and the warp and weft threads are usually made of pre-spun and treated cotton. In very large enterprises, more like factories than the early, small workshop arrangement, the wool is sometimes dyed and spun on the premises using the latest machine spinning techniques and dyeing methods. In some small workshops the wool is still hand spun and dyed but usually the base threads are purchased ready for use and are mostly made of cotton. The vertical loom is almost always used in a workshop situation.

Workshop rugs come from most production areas today although the output from some centres seems to suggest that the term 'factory' would be more suitable. There is considerable output in many areas of Pakistan, most of India, parts of Turkey and Iran, the USSR and China. Small workshops offer the best chance of obtaining an individual item and these can be found in some Turkish rural centres, areas of Iran, some Kashmiri centres or small businesses in Pakistan and India and some Tibetan co-operatives in Nepal and India.

Weaver's tools—graphed design, scissors and comb as used in small workshops (4 to 6 vertical looms at each site) in Karachi suburbs, 1989

Village Carpets

The term 'village carpets' is used to describe rugs which were produced by isolated village dwelling groups from local wool, spun and dyed in the village using local vegetable dyes, and knotted in a particular style with designs which were traditional and handed down from family to family, so evolving and making it possible to date specific examples.

Some modern rugs are still produced in village situations but many designs are created by entrepreneurs who utilise motifs which are traditional to the area; wool is usually spun and supplied to individual households and looms are mass produced and supplied to the sub-contract workers who knot the rugs in their homes for payment on completion. These modern village made rugs are available from areas of Turkey, Iran and Afghanistan, and even though there have been vast changes in the production from all these areas, it is hoped that semi-traditional items will continue to be made in this environment.

Tribal Carpets

Tribal rugs were made by isolated tribes or clans of nomads who roamed the Central Asian steppes, Afghanistan, Baluchistan, parts of Iran and eastern Turkey. The earliest surviving examples I have seen date from the late eighteenth century and desirable collectors' pieces come from the mid to late nineteenth century.

The base weave was always wool or a wool and hair mix, the pile nearly always wool although sometimes a small amount of silk can be found in the designs. The wool was hand spun and plied, dyed and knotted by the members of individual tribes usually on horizontal looms made from any wood that could be found. Designs were often learnt in the form of a song (the words would be like 'two reds and then two blues, seven reds and another two blues', etc.) which were passed from mother to daughter or, later, young weavers in the tribe would set up their looms above their mother's rug and try to copy the design.

Weaver beating the wefts after completing some rows of pile knots. Karachi, 1989

Many tribes had no written language and the only items left for the modern world to study are their rugs, knotted and woven household items and clothing. Usually their tents were woven goat hair or felted wool and everything they used in their everyday life was made by the members of the tribe. Through a study of structural details and design evolution it is possible to estimate quite accurately the age of most tribal rugs.

Few modern tribal rugs are made as there are very few tribal groups left who live a traditional lifestyle and have the skills and materials to spontaneously create hand knotted or woven handicrafts. The majority of new rugs made by tribal people which are available today have been made in village situations and these can be called either by their ethnic origins or the geographic location of the production centre.

Large Uzbek kilim, 3.9 X 1.9 m. Slitwoven and double interlocking tapestry approximately 30 years old from the Maimana area of north-west Afghanistan. Author's collection

MODERN ORIENTAL CARPETS

The production of oriental carpets is a very large industry and, in some developing countries, plays a major role in the economy. Often the wool used for the pile is imported and in many cases there are inputs into the industry from Western market advisers and researchers as well as designers and entrepreneurs. The present situation seems a logical evolution from the older, more traditional occurrence in the production of rugs when wealthy or powerful leaders would buy wool then organise a dyemaster, designer and weavers to make carpets.

The major difference in modern production is that the output is intended specifically for resale and export. In many cases designs are reproduced en masse in large factories and in standard sizes and colours, making the finished item a very commercial product. In assessing new rugs it is important to take into account the reasons for purchase and to decide on an object's merit in terms of durability and usefulness in a specific situation as well as estimating the comparable costs and value for money.

I have tried to arrange the major rug producing countries and their present output in a way that will make it easy for the reader to understand the production methods used in these areas as well as to recognise a rug from a specific country. I also hope that by organising the information in this way it will be easier for the reader to decide on the individual merit of hand made carpets from various geographical centres and to understand the work and organisation that was required to place a new carpet in one of the many showrooms to be found in almost every city of the world.

There are problems when information is classified by geographical area and the reader must remember that national borders are, in many cases, arbitrary lines drawn across a map which can divide ethnic groups in a very unnatural manner. The handicrafts of these groups can retain very similar techniques and styles and the modern-day nation in which they are made has little bearing on the quality or value of the product.

A region where an overlapping in style occurs even though the rugs were made in different countries is the Baluchistan province of Pakistan, where the handicrafts of Baluch and other tribal groups are very similar in structure and production techniques to their counterparts from the southeast of Afghanistan and Iran.

It must also be noted that the term 'new rugs' refers to carpets which have been made but have not yet been sold to a consumer. Since this is a relatively long term industry which is based in many remote countries with often unstable politics, it is not unusual for carpets to be stored in warehouses, either in the country of origin or some other transit point for a number of years before finally finding their way into a Western dealer's retail showroom. Other rugs which are described in this section may have been used for up to fifty years before being offered for resale but, because of the environment of manufacture, the place they were made, the type of dyes used or the people who made them, are not suitable for inclusion in any sort of collectable or 'antique' grouping and are usually offered for sale in a 'new' carpet outlet.

4 Carpets from Afghanistan

The carpets of Afghanistan were the last major group to be exploited by Western markets and this is probably because of the remote position of many of the weavers as well as the unique lifestyles and beliefs of the many tribal groups who inhabit the country. When any were offered for sale they were usually called simply 'Afghans' or 'Baluch' and little work was done in classifying individual ethnic, tribal or geographically separate weaving groups until the 1970s.

It is my belief that many tribal weavers continued to spontaneously create carpets in a traditional living environment and using design motifs and patterns that were part of the memory of the weaver until as late as the 1950s. Semi-nomadic tribal groups and the mixed ethnic populations of many isolated villages continued to produce carpets from local wool and in traditional patterns and designs for longer and dealers like Leigh and Alexandra Copeland, who first visited the country in the early 1970s, have observed small village and tribal groups weaving in a traditional environment.

In organising the carpets from Afghanistan I have used the knowledge gained from almost ten years' involvement with the Copelands and many hours of conversation about the fascinating people and handicrafts of Afghanistan, as well as from my personal interactions with Afghan refugees and the weavings they have sold since the early 1980s in the Northwest Frontier and Baluchistan province of Pakistan.

Tribal Rugs

There are many tribal groups in Afghanistan and a major percentage of handicrafts produced in the last thirty years were made with hand spun wool from the local region. Primitive dyeing techniques, often using some vegetable dyes, and traditional design motifs were also employed. I have tried to distinguish between rug types without compromising my production classifications. The tribal groups listed in this section have created hand woven and knotted handicrafts in an isolated, nomadic or semi-nomadic environment and their products can be found in the market place at present. Many of the rugs for sale are more than fifteen years old although they have never been used by a consumer, and since the mid 1970s there has been an increase in older items for sale.

Many Afghan households had to sell their personal possessions as a result of the Russian interference in their country and in most retail outlets for Afghan rugs at present there is at least a minor representation of these older goods. Prior to 1980 no rugs made in Afghanistan used cotton as a base weave and all the wool used for carpets was produced and hand spun within the country.

Over the last couple of years, however, I have noticed that a few new pieces, most commercially organised, have had cotton warp threads. Others have contained very fine, machine spun wool which looked like an imported product. These have been in the vast minority but are an indication that the rugs to be made in Afghanistan, if production ever manages to reach pre-Soviet proportions again, will not be the same as those made there before the war.

Baluch

There is a wide range of Baluch and Baluch type production in Afghanistan and I have seen prayer rugs which appear to have been made in a nomadic environment offered for sale in all the retail centres I have visited. This type of piece was still made only twenty years ago and I believe that many of the rugs made at that time are still being offered for sale in Eastern markets.

'Baluch' is a very broad category of rugs and even in Afghanistan there is a large variety of items covered by the

Carpet repair stall in Peshawar, Pakistan, 1984

Old Taimani pile rug, 2.8 × 1.45 m. Early 20th century from Afghanistan. An aniline dye used in some areas of the pile can be seen as an abrash in the field where it has faded dramatically. Author's collection

name: kilims and storage bags in weft brocade technique, and knotted pile, dark coloured rugs tightly knotted on finely spun woollen warps, prayer rugs in reds, blues and browns and large carpets in a variety of designs. When choosing a Baluch piece, check construction details—whether the sides are exactly parallel, the dyes a constant colour throughout the rug, the design symmetrical, the motifs used the same shape in each instance, what materials are used in the warp and weft and how the fibres are spun—in order to ascertain if it was made in a primitive tribal setting or produced in some more organised and commercial endeavour, as the name is also used to describe a number of rugs made in a sub-contract village environment.

Nearly all Baluch rugs from Afghanistan are knotted with an asymmetrical knot on a hand spun woollen base. The density of knots per square inch can vary from about 40 to 150 and the variety of wool used in the pile is diverse.

Taimani

The Taimani are a Baluch-related group who live on large tracts of tribal land in the Farah and Ghor provinces of Afghanistan. Most of the population live in tents and move with their flocks in search of grass throughout the year. During the cold winter months the moving population gathers in many mud-walled villages and towns which are the permanent bases for the tribe.

They produce pile rugs which are asymmetrically knotted, usually to no more than 50 knots per square inch, with a hand spun warp and weft. The knots tend to have a flattish feel and there are usually no warps depressed on

Old Taimani prayer rug, 1.1 X 0.95 m. Early 20th century from Afghanistan. The Lindley Collection

the back of the rug. The pile is at least 10 mm long and often includes very coarse wool fibres, sometimes even goat hair. The warps and wefts are often spun with a mixture of materials and goat, camel or horse hair can be included.

The main colours used include some vegetable dyed red and mauve tones, orange and the occasional green of obvious chemical origin, sometimes light blue and a range of earthy brown, fawn, black, beige and white tones from the undyed wool of their flocks. All have geometric motifs, usually in a repeat pattern. Occasionally, large octagons are used in the main field and diamond-shaped flowers can be found in the borders. Many small prayer rugs which are

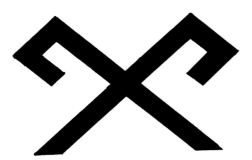

Small ram's horn motif

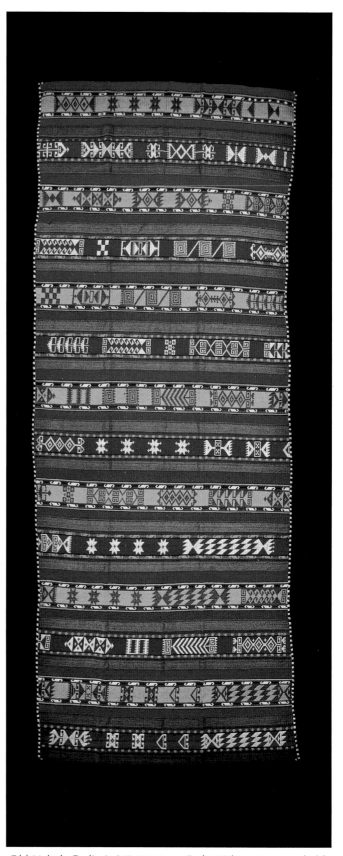

Old Uzbek Gadjeri, 3.7 X 1.4 m. Early 20th century, probably from the Hindu Kush region in the far north-east of Afghanistan. Author's collection

made show the ram's horn motif atop the mihrab and are usually in soft red tones combined with natural browns, fawn, black and blue. Older pieces often display a square mihrab and are coloured only in red and blue tones.

I am of the opinion that the dyeing techniques used are not well refined and in some pieces I have studied the colour has not taken to the fibres sufficiently, suggesting an ineffective mordant was used during the dyeing process, or none at all. In many cases this gives the rug a unique appeal as the different dyelots used throughout the rug show different tones of the same colour and add depth to the design.

Taimani rugs are hard wearing, easy to wash and produced in a primitive environment; most range in size from about 1.2 × 0.6 m to 3.0 × 1.8 m.

Uzbek

The origin of the Uzbek tribes of Central Asia is thought to have been the Mongol invasion of the region at the end of the thirteenth century. However, by the late nineteenth century few Uzbeks lived a nomadic existence in Turkestan. By 1911, when the government of Turkestan held census, there were approximately 1.8 million Uzbeks in the newly

Old Uzbek cradle, approximately 1.0 × 0.5 × 0.5 m. First half of the 20th century, probably from the Hindu Kush region in the far north-east of Afghanistan. Author's collection

formed Trans-Caspian States. Most of these led settled lives as merchants or artisans in the towns of Turkestan but a percentage had moved to the north of Afghanistan and have lived a nomadic or semi-nomadic existence there until very recently.

These groups were scattered across the northern border of Afghanistan and stretched from Maimana in the west to Faizalabad in the east. Many of the descendants of these original groups have settled in towns in this area but large numbers of Uzbeks have lived a semi-nomadic way of life, weaving tribal kilims from the wool of their own flocks, until modern times.

Uzbek kilims are usually slit-woven or double interlocked and often both techniques are seen in the same piece. The warps are almost always a grey coloured wool or wool and hair mix, the dyes often include some of vegetable origin and they are hard wearing, earthy looking kilims which ideally suit a relaxed living environment. They appear in a range of sizes from approx. 1 × 2 m to 5 × 2.5 m. The design is often made up of large stepped diamond shapes which vary in proportion from almost square to thin and elongated. They sometimes cover the whole kilim without any border surrounding them. Another common motif is a very large diamond with hooked ends which is set like a medallion in the field and surrounded by a border of large geometric, 'S' shapes. More unusual is a design of 'arrowheads' arranged on the rug in rows. These vary in width from 10 to 20 cm and are usually interspersed with stripes of plain weave. A wide variety of colours is seen but red, blue, white and natural tones of wool are common and some kilims contain orange, dark blue or mauve.

I have also seen a wide range of Uzbek household trappings which include small silk, cotton or rayon cross-stitch embroideries, felted and plainweave woollen rugs with embroidered patterning, and hand woven decorative strips which are used as tent straps (to hold the tent up) and as internal decorations. These strips are usually no more than 30 cm wide and made in a type of warp float weaving method. They are seen in lengths of up to 15 metres and a type of Uzbek kilim known as Gadjeri is produced by cutting a long strip into lengths, binding the loose warps of individual sections then stitching these narrow strips together to form a rug size section of weaving which is usually bound around the edges with a very narrow selvedge.

Hazara

The Hazara are another tribal group of Central Asian origin. They live in mountainous central Afghanistan and can be found from Hazarajat, in the south, to Bamiyan, in the north. Although they are a relatively small tribal group they have a fierce reputation and their name, which comes from the word hazar, meaning thousand, is said to have been given to them by the frightened occupants of the villages their ancestors pillaged when first they came to Afghanistan.

Detail of Hazara kilim, 3.94 × 2.1 m. Weft brocade technique. Second half of the 20th century, central Afghanistan. Author's collection

The band is said to have been only one thousand strong yet it quickly defeated all opponents and when a villager saw the tribe bearing down on them he would shout 'the Hazar', the thousand, as a warning to his neighbours. The Hazara now are mostly farmers who own small numbers of sheep and graze them in the rugged mountains which are their home. The kilims of the Hazara can be divided into two distinct groups. The first are woven by the double interlocking tapestry technique and mainly appear in long, thin sizes. My research has shown that most of these come from the more northern areas.

The second are often large in size, sometimes more than 3 × 2 m, and use a floating weft brocade technique. These come mainly from Hazarajat. The output of this group is minimal; the pieces which appear on the market are usually of fine quality and display clear colours and intricate design motifs.

I believe that the kilims I have seen for sale are at least fifteen years old and could well be older, even though they show no signs of having been used in a household environment. I have found no evidence of post-Russian production of these pieces and suspect that none have been made since the late 1970s. The once easy to obtain, large (to 2 × 1 m) flat-woven quorjin associated with this group are now not often seen.

Turkoman

There are many Turkoman-related tribal groups in Afghanistan. Both the Yomud and Ersari subgroups are represented but I have found it more convenient to list their carpets in the village production section of this book. In doing this I am not questioning their ethnic background but drawing conclusions about the ways in which their rugs are produced, the source of supply of the wool and dyes, the design techniques and the environment in which the weavers knot the carpets.

I think these considerations make the products of the Turkomen in Afghanistan more a village than a tribal craft. Another major reason for classifying the rugs in this way is to try to distinguish between the production in different regions by naming them after the towns and villages in which they are made.

Village Rugs

Most of the population of Afghanistan, no matter what lifestyle they lead, are of tribal origin. I have often been introduced to someone then told of their ethnic background as a matter of course. Most Afghans are fiercely proud of their tribal origins and I have no wish to undermine this loyalty by listing the production of certain areas of the country in this section rather than under a tribal grouping.

I have done so in order to divide the weavings into more easily recognised categories and because I feel that the way the rugs have been made is more suited to this classification. Some of the rugs made by the tribal groups I have listed may also have been produced in a more village type environment, as indeed some of those in my village category may have been made by a nomadic group; this is always the case when trying to classify oriental rugs.

Oriental rugs are uniquely individual items and whenever one tries to organise a group of weavings there is bound to be one that does not conform to the rules established for classification. The student must accept this anomaly and carry on regardless.

There is a large group of rugs made in villages in the north of Afghanistan that show obvious Turkoman influence. They are usually coloured deep red with blue or black designs, use large octagons as the major field ornament, are knotted with hand spun wool on a hand spun wool warp and weft using an asymmetrical knot and vary in size from about 2 × 1 m to over 3 × 2 m.

A major group are known as Suleyman and this name refers to an Ersari Turkoman subgroup. These usually include some extra patterning in the flat-weave ends, the serrated leaf, flower stem or comb motif in the main octagons and a variety of minor ornaments.

Kunduz

The town of Kunduz, in the far north-east of Afghanistan, has never been a major rug producing centre but the inhabitants of nearby villages bring their weavings to the markets there and the name has come to be associated with the carpets made in the region.

It has been reported that some Pashtun tribal groups living in this region make pile front baleshts and storage bags but most of the carpets made near Kunduz are produced by ethnic Turkomans of the Ersari subgroup and are usually included in the Suleyman group. They are the finest and most sought after of this type of rug and almost always have some finely worked, extra weft wrapping, usually in bright red, blue, white and the very occasional yellow, included in the flat-woven end treatments.

The carpets have a red coloured ground, usually a rich, dark colour, and are patterned in dark blue or black. The major ornament is a large octagon or *gul* which is repeated in rows on the main field. This gul is usually quartered and contains the serrated leaf or pine tree motif. Minor design ornaments vary and the borders usually contain geometric shapes and small *boteh* or paisley shapes.

An asymmetrical knot is used in the pile, usually to a density of about 80 knots per square inch, and the wool is of a very durable quality. They are found in sizes from about 2 × 0.8 m to 4 × 2.6 m. I do not know of any current production in the region but have seen a variety of unused rugs which would have been made in the last fifteen years.

Section of major border commonly seen in Suleyman rugs from the Aq Char and Chakesh regions of Afghanistan

Aq Char

The production from the Aq Char region, in the northwest of the country, is not thought to be of as good a quality as from Kunduz but there are many finely drawn, coloured and knotted rugs made in the region. The makers are again of Turkoman-related, Suleyman origin and their rugs show only red, blue and black colours. The main design gul used is often quite stiffly drawn and the quartered octagon often shows four small flower heads in its centre. The main border design is usually made up of bold diamond shapes and the minor borders utilise a variety of geometric shapes.

The rugs made in nearby **Chakesh** are also included in this group and these always have a diamond shaped motif in the centre of the main gul. The most common size is 3 × 2 m and an asymmetrical knot is used to tie the pile to a density not usually greater than 70 knots per square inch. The warp threads are hand spun grey wool and the warp ends in a typical piece show a small strip of plainweave and are then tied together at regular intervals across the fringe.

Andkhoy

The town of Andkhoy is the centre of production for a number of rug weaving groups. The major population groups are again of Turkoman descent but should be divided into the Suleyman and another Ersari-related group which has been called the Charchangi. Although both groups usually use only red, blue and black colours and the weaving styles are very similar, the products vary greatly in design.

The Andkhoy Suleyman contains large octagons in the field and is usually enclosed by a number of borders. This tends to make the rug look a little cluttered in design and is probably one of the reasons why these pieces are

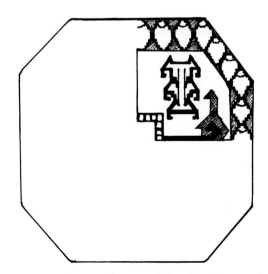

One quarter of Suleyman design gul showing 'pine tree' motif which is commonly seen in rugs from the Kunduz region of northern Afghanistan.

Design gul commonly seen in rugs from the Chakesh region of Afghanistan. Mr and Mrs Lehman

Baluch prayer rug, 1.2 × 0.8 m. From Afghanistan. Author's collection

Baluch storage bag from Afghanistan. Author's collection

Old Kyzil Ayak prayer rug, 1.0 × 0.7 m. First half of the 20th century from the region around Kyzil Ayak, in the north of Afghanistan. The Lindley Collection

considered the most inferior quality of Suleyman rugs. The wool used is of good quality, the asymmetrical knot is used to tie the pile and they can be found in a range of sizes.

The rugs of the Charchangi often contain small, geometric S type borders as well as the more common geometric flower motifs. The central field is designed with guls that have pointed edges and are very delicately drawn; these are interspersed with rows of bold diamond shapes which contain elegant geometric scrolls and flowers. An asymmetrical knot is used to tie the pile and the density is usually no more than 60 knots per square inch. The main colours are red and blue or black but small areas of white are also seen.

Saltuqs

Another group of weavers who lived in Afghan Turkestan are known as the Saltuqs. These descendants of Turkic people produced rugs in the Andkhoy, Labijar and Aq Char regions and their products can be distinguished by the use of white in the border stripes combined with a running dog motif. The major design guls vary in form and the colours used include red, blue, small amounts of yellow and white. Few rugs from this group have been made in the last thirty years; most modern weavings are named after the place of production and cannot be distinguished from the other products of the area. Older pieces can be found and these are usually very durable and attractive. A fine example appears on page 8.

Qarqueen

The region around this town in the north of Afghanistan, very close to the Soviet border, is home to more Turkoman-related groups who weave rugs of a different style to the Suleyman. The carpets are often only found in smaller sizes and the weave is much looser, giving the rug a less stiff feel than most north Afghan production. The asymmetrical knot is used and the main colours are red, blue, black and white.

In older pieces vegetable dyes are common and many rugs utilise the large octagon as the major ornament. I have seen prayer rugs called Qarqueen with pictures of a mosque in the main field as well as small rugs with an all over repeat design.

Kyzil Ayak

Kyzil Ayak is the name of a town near Andkhoy as well as the name of an Ersari Turkoman subtribe and the description when used for a rug is often confusing. The most common items labelled as Kyzil Ayak show an asymmetrical knot which is indented on one side. This can be seen on the back of the rug as every alternate warp thread is depressed. They are often in prayer rug sizes and I have seen many which include pictures of mosques or other buildings. The smaller examples, to 1 × 0.7 m, typically show the ram's horn motif atop a triangular mihrab which encloses one or more geometric motifs on a plain red field.

The warp materials are of fine, hand spun wool and the colours used include blue, red, white and occasionally small areas of yellow. Most of the examples I have seen appear to be at least thirty years old, some even older, and show obvious signs of use on the floor in Afghanistan before being offered for sale.

Herat

Herat is the major trading centre for village produced rugs from the west of Afghanistan and the variety is diverse. Many Baluch type rugs are sold there and a number of items commercially produced in the region are offered for sale at the present time in Pakistan. From my research I believe that so far most of these enterprises have been run in a cottage industry situation where villagers knot the carpets in their homes.

Some of the recent (made in the last ten years) production includes a number of 'War Rugs' which depict helicopter gun ships, rifles, jets and cannons in the designs. Others include more traditional designs and are nearly always made on a hand spun woollen base with an asymmetrical knot. Some of the finer quality of Baluch style rugs made in this region contain up to 200 knots per square inch.

During 1990 I saw a few pieces which were said to have come from Herat and were woven on a cotton base and appeared very commercial, so it is possible that in the near future the production from this area will be organised in more of a workshop environment instead of the traditional village setting, if indeed this is not already the case.

5 Carpets from Turkey

Turkey is one of the major rug producing countries in the world, having a healthy export industry which supplies all the larger Western outlets as well as a thriving domestic market and large demand from the international tourists who visit the country. It is common for the name Anatolia to be used when describing carpets and this is quite adequate as it is the local name for the part of the country which lies east of the Bosphorus and includes all major rug producing areas.

The carpet industry has developed in two vastly different directions. The large, established centres of mass production, such as Kayseri, have grown, supplying increasing numbers of woollen pile, curvilinear designed carpets in wider size and colour ranges, as well as developing silk and floss silk (mercerised) rugs in larger ranges of pattern and quality. At the same time as this broad, consumer-based output has increased, European and American collector interest has been aroused by the revival in traditional village-produced items, woven from hand spun wool, dyed with vegetable products and using antique rugs from the local region as a basis for designs.

The steady, organised production of woollen pile rugs knotted to a woollen base and the more spontaneous kilim weaving from major country centres have also continued and there is a large range of well made, durable rugs to be found.

Tribal Rugs

The tribal rugs produced in Turkey are usually called *kurds* or *yoruk*. The latter is a word which means nomad to most Turks I have spoken to but also refers to a specific antique, tribal rug group. It is difficult to gauge the amount of weaving which is done by the large number of nomads of Kurdish origin who live in Turkey. There is no doubt that primitive

groups continue to weave and some of their new products appear in the Istanbul bazaar and Western sales rooms.

Most modern pieces are brightly coloured, coarsely knotted on a cotton or woollen base, use primitive design motifs and are described by the region in which they were made or by the name of a specific tribal subgroup. Many are presented as old items when offered for sale in the bazaar and some are no doubt more than twenty years old, even though they appear to be in unused condition. Most are more suited to a village classification although some conform to traditional Kurdish tribal rugs which are described in the antique section of this book.

Village Carpets

There are two main areas of village production operating at present in Turkey. The first is a long-term, organised output from a number of geographic areas, the products of which have been seen on the market over the last twenty years in steady numbers and in recognisable types. Within a specific type, similar design motifs, format, colour layout and balance can be seen, although some pieces show an individuality which displays a level of personal input from the makers.

A disappointing aspect of this first area of production is the growing trend among Turkish merchants to chemically wash the finished product in an attempt to market the rug as an old item at an inflated price or to give the pile a more lustrous appearance. Most of the rugs treated in this way that I have seen are not heavily washed and the natural resilience of the wool fibres has not been completely negated, but I have also seen Turkish carpets that have been severely damaged by a strong bleach or alkalis.

The second level of new production has seen considerable input from Western sources whose motives were to revive the traditional spinning, dyeing and weaving skills which had very strong links with specific geographical areas. Projects begun by Western scholars, rug collectors and dealers in an attempt to revive the quality and beauty of the rugs from Turkey's past have succeeded in gaining a strong following from the buying public and there are a number of weavers in different geographical centres operating at present.

Melas

Rugs known as Melas are usually long and thin in size and not normally larger than 2.5 × 1.2 m. The wool pile is tied with a symmetrical knot, on a wool warp, to a density no greater than 70 knots per square inch. There is a range of colours available and I have seen rugs containing orange, red, blue, brown and white as well as the more common dusty brown, yellow, white and beige tones. All dyes used appear to be of chemical origin.

The design motifs and layout are based on those traditionally used in the region, which is in the south-west of the country, and usually contain a long, narrow-shaped field and have vaguely triangular forms in the wide surrounding borders.

The production of Melas rugs is obviously organised and it seems as if weavers work from a graphed design which has been supplied by the organiser, but I believe much of the weaving takes place in the homes of the makers and I have seen some which show individual design elements or colour arrangement. They are available in most retail outlets in Turkey and Western centres and have a good reputation for durability when they have not been treated with strong chemicals.

Kula

Kula is the name of a town situated inland from the large port city of Izmir. The type of rug which commonly bears this designation is made with a symmetrical knot on a woollen base and often is designed in the form of a prayer rug. The pile is quite long and the knot density varies between about 30 and 60 per square inch. An occasional cotton-warped rug named after the nearby town of Ghiordes can also be found and these are knotted in designs which are vague reproductions of antique rugs from the area.

The colours are usually derived from chemical dyes and the patterns show a stiff form; these rugs should not be confused with the antique rugs which bear the same names. Some of the modern production is of a good durable quality and some of the designs I have seen are pleasant, but I have also found many rugs of this type made with inferior materials or heavily faded by artificial means.

Doseamalti

Another common group of available rugs are called Doseamalti and they appear in colours of red, blue and

Detail of a Doseamalti pile rug, 1.75 × 1.2 m. Modern production showing intricate design and subtle colour combinations. The Lindley Collection

Old piled front saddle bags of Doseamalti origin. First half of the 20th century. Photographed in a way which excludes the approximately 20 cm long, flat-woven central panel. M. and G. Drummond

white, occasionally combining pleasing greenish tones and very dark blues. They are found in runners, to about 3.5 m in length, and in a rectangular format of about 1.8 × 1.2 m.

Kars area—bus bogged in snow, 1985

Wayside village close to Bitlis, near Lake Van, 1985

Modern Turkish saddle bag. Author's collection

The designs include triangular medallions, usually heavily serrated or scrolled in appearance.

A symmetrical knot, tied to a woollen warp and sometimes slightly indented on one side, is used to a density of about 80 per square inch and the wool in the pile is of a good quality. There are many rugs of this type for sale and most are very similar in quality and appearance. When viewing large numbers I have seen examples that do not conform to the normal output and this is usually because of a different type of wool being used in the pile or the inclusion of some greenish-blue dyes or a more subtle mix of colours.

It is obvious that the production is well organised, in many cases having a uniformity of design, size and colours. They appear to have been made in a workshop environment and some of the output is chemically washed, but there are large numbers of well made, very durable and appealing rugs of this type which can be found.

Yah Yali

Rugs known as Yah Yali come in three sizes from about 1.8 × 0.7 m to 3 × 1.4 m and almost always have the same basic design format which consists of a triangular-ended central field containing a large angular medallion, the central portion of which often contains a hooked lozenge, 'tarantula' type motif. The wide main border is usually designed with geometric shapes and the main colours are red, blue, brown, dark green and white and the dyes all appear to be of chemical origin.

A symmetrical knot is used to tie the pile to a density of no more than about 70 per square inch and one side of the knot is usually slightly depressed. The base is of woollen construction, often the warps being hand spun, and the weft threads are often dyed red. I have seen many which have been slightly washed and the pile has a slightly unnatural sheen. The rugs are said to come from villages around Nigde in central Turkey.

Kars

Kars is a large town in the mountains of north-east Turkey, close to the border of the USSR. The region is remote and inhospitable and was once part of the Armenian empire. Most of the population are peasant farmers or soldiers, conscripted into the army and training in the many army camps which can be seen in the region.

The rugs which are known by this name are thickly piled and use a symmetrical knot on a woollen base, which in most cases is hand spun. The knot density is not usually greater than about 50 per square inch and the knot appears to be squarish in appearance when viewed from the back of the rug. Multiple wefts are common and the rugs have a thick and heavy feel. Geometrical shapes with hooked lozenges are common and many are made in the style of the Sewan Kazak group of rugs made during the nineteenth century in the southern Caucasus. There is a wide range of colours available, from red, blue and white combinations to tones of dark red, green, brown and fawn and they appeal to a broad section of consumers.

I have seen many recently which have had the black lines in the design trimmed low, to imitate an oxidising effect, and the other colours chemically faded in order for them to be marketed as an old or antique piece. It is usually easy to pick these as the dye fades much more on the ends of the pile and if you look at the base of the knot it will be a different colour from the tips of the pile.

Although the production of Kars rugs is obviously organised to some degree, there are a number of rugs made which show a propensity of design and format that is very charming in a new carpet.

Kilims are also named after this centre and from my observations they mostly utilise the slitwoven tapestry method of weaving. They are usually quite large, up to 4 or 5 m × 2 m, have geometric designs often centring around bold, squarish medallions and the most common colours are brown, blue, white and sometimes small areas of pink. The weavings of this type are quite thick and heavy and, although loosely woven, are very durable.

Van

The frontier town of Van is in the east of Turkey on a major route into Iran. The kilims woven in the region are said to be made by Kurdish people but it is difficult to discover more than the fact that they are made by the peasant workers on many of the large landholdings in the area. The traditional Van area kilim contains small diamond patterns arranged in rows across the rug and was often made in two narrow pieces which were stitched together when completed in order to create a wider rug.

As well as these traditional types I have seen kilims woven in the manner of Bijar and Senneh, in Iran, using the same design and slitwoven style of weaving as well as colours and materials.

Kilims

There are many modern kilims available that have been woven in a village environment in a number of areas of Turkey. These pieces usually use the slitwoven tapestry technique or cicim style embroidery and are named after a large village or town in the region of their production. Some were obviously made in the past even though they appear unused when offered for sale and they are seen in a variety of forms.

Small coverlets, cushions (commonly known as yastiks), storage bags and saddle bags as well as prayer kilims and large room-size floor coverings are available and some display a primitive charm and appeal that is unique to Turkish weavings. New items usually include chemical dyes and many of them have been artificially faded in an attempt

Modern Turkish kilim, 2.0 × 1.1 m. John Leach Tribal Rug and
Kilim Gallery

to represent them as older pieces, but in most cases this
process does not diminish their durability.

A large group of new kilims to be found are produced
in and around Kayseri and are woven in the slitwoven
tapestry technique. The colours are usually bright and can
contain dyes that are not fixed properly and will run when
the rug is first washed, others have been heavily sun faded
or bleached and the colours have lost their definition.

The Dobag Project

In the early 1980s the first of a number of lectures and
vegetable dyeing demonstrations was given to a group of
villagers who lived in the region around Ayvalik, on the coast
of western Turkey. These educational sessions were the
practical culmination of many years of research into dyeing
techniques, traditional dyestuffs and vegetable dyeing
'recipes' by a German academic named Harold Bohmer
who had worked in Turkey since the 1960s. They were also
the first steps in reviving the traditional weaving and dyeing

skills of the area and were made possible by a development
project called Dogal Boya Arastirma ve Gelistirme Projesi,
commonly called the Dobag project.

The area of western Anatolia chosen contained a number
of towns which had been centres for distribution of highly
regarded rugs more than a century ago and the population
of the many tiny settlements which dotted the range of
rugged coastal hills was still involved in spontaneous rug
weaving, although most output was for domestic use and
of very little value on the Western market. It was also a
growing coastal tourist centre—Ayvalik is situated on the
main coast road between Isanbul and Izmir and is only an
hour's boat ride from the Greek island of Lesbos. Cannakale
provides a perfect overnight stop on the same highway as
the bus must cross the Dardanelles at this point, and the
scenic hillsides offer pine forests, cool streams and ancient
archaeological sites—and also provided good access to the
Western market for a unique new Turkish product.

Herr Bohmer visited many villages and distributed printed
instructions written in basic Turkish and illustrated with line
drawings together with the natural ingredients to produce
a range of basic colours. He demonstrated how to dye the
wool and the villagers went home to try it out. The weavers
were, in many cases, still using their traditional designs and
when the first rugs began to appear it was obvious that the
Dobag project was on the right track.

The output soon found a market in the West and a rug
co-operative was formed to organise distribution and sale
of completed rugs from individual weavers. The environment was established for the individual creation of a carpet
in a primitive environment and using traditional designs,
which in some cases had been taught to a young girl by
her mother before the project was begun.

Rugs from this region are now exported throughout the
world and the project has expanded to other geographic
locations. Other interest groups have been formed and
weavers contracted to make vegetable dyed rugs in a variety
of designs and most of this type of output is named after
the group or organisation responsible for its production.

Workshop Carpets

Kayseri

The city of Kayseri has been a major centre for carpets made
in a workshop situation for more than a century. The designs
woven are either of classic 'Persian' origin with many flowery
spandrels and curvilinear designs or poor copies of old
Turkish rugs. The symmetrical knot is used to tie the pile,
which is either wool, silk or mercerised cotton—often called
floss silk—and the base weave is cotton.

There are a number of different knot densities, the finest
being those rugs made with a silk pile. Most of the woollen
piled rugs are chemically washed and it is necessary when

Old West Anatolian Cicim, 1.0 × 1.1 m. First half of the 20th century. The Lindley Collection

Left: *Old Cannakale prayer rug, 0.9 × 0.6 m. First half of the 20th century.* The Lindley Collection

Shop front near the Grand Bazaar, Instanbul, showing some Kayseri, multiple mihrab, piled prayer rugs hanging on the side and very top of doorway

looking at Kayseri rugs to find those which have been left in the most natural state. The silk used in the pile of Kayseri rugs is usually of a good quality but be sure to compare the materials with those rugs made to imitate silk to be sure the product you are viewing contains natural spun silk.

As in most workshop situations there is a wide variety of designs, qualities and colour ranges, and rugs from this region are exported in very large numbers to all major trading centres as the diverse patterns, colours and styles have a broad commercial appeal.

Hereke

Hereke rugs are among the most finely knotted silk piled rugs made in the world today. The designs used are curvilinear and some can be found which contain small areas of gold or metal thread embroidery. The bulk of the silk piled rugs are knotted to a silk warp and have a silk weft but there are different combinations made. Wool piled rugs are sometimes knotted on a silk warp and include silk piled highlights in the design and some of the less densely knotted carpets I have seen used cotton for a warp or weft material.

Most are in small prayer rug formats, usually smaller than 1.8 X 1 m, and there is a wide variety of chemically dyed colours to choose from. The knot count varies from about 200 to 700 per square inch and the finest pieces are sought after and expensive both in Turkey and through Western retail outlets, although they are wholesaled at a square metre price in the same manner as most commercial weavings in Turkey.

6 Carpets from Iran

The country of Iran is the centre of what was the ancient Persian Empire which at one time controlled almost all of Asia Minor and whose influence stretched from Greece to India. The earliest history of carpet weaving in this area is obscure but it is known that large, finely knotted, curvilinear designed carpets, were produced during the sixteenth century and some survive to this day. The Ardabil carpet in the Victoria and Albert Museum measures more than 10 metres in length and its origin has been traced to this period in the city of Kashan.

When assessing the bulk of the finely knotted, curvilinear designed weavings produced in Iran attention is usually devoted to more mundane details such as the type of materials used, the durability and functionality of the individual item and its comparative value when viewed alongside the output from other areas of the world.

Examples I have viewed, which appear to have been made during the last twenty years, can be grouped into two major types. The first shows the characteristics of production in a village or very small co-operative environment and includes coarsely knotted, longer piled rugs made by settled or semi-nomadic tribal groups and the output from remote villages in many parts of Iran. The other rug type is usually finely knotted, appears in specific sizes, colour and design types and is obviously produced in a well organised and substantial workshop environment.

It must also be noted that the output of carpets was affected by the deposition of the most recent Shah and the later war with Iraq. There is a marked difference between many carpets made before the mid 1970s and those made in the late 1980s and a temporary oversupply on the Western market caused by the rush of goods from the country during the early political turmoil seems to have diminished. When preparing the listings for this group of rugs I have included some common rug types and a guide to the qualities in which they appear.

Iran has a major input into the oriental carpet industry and there are carpets from Iran available in all Australian, Asian and European cities. There are a number of individual types and styles available and they appeal to a broad range of consumers. The chemical treatment of carpets is common and most carpets exported from the country have been 'washed' to some degree. Most weavings are durable although care must be taken to choose carpets whose dyes do not run or fade. Carpets from Iran can be used in all domestic situations.

Tribal Rugs

The major tribal groups from Iran are listed in the antiques section of this book. This is not intended to be a judgement about the age of all surviving tribal rugs but about the rarity and inherent collectability of most spontaneously produced tribal weavings from the country. I have found it easier to refer to present day carpet production in terms of the geographical area in which it occurred and have included any information which relates to the tribal background of the makers in the appropriate section.

There is no doubt that tribal groups still survive in Iran and that many lead a traditional lifestyle but I have based this book on the 'new' rug market as I have experienced it and have made assumptions about the level of involvement of the entrepreneur in the actual design and production of different types of carpets in order to use the most appropriate classification for the items I have chosen to include.

From the production I have viewed, which in most cases appears in specific sizes, approximate knot densities, design styles and colours, it seems likely that the carpets made in recent times are produced in an environment which is more suitable to the village classification, even though there seems to be little doubt that there is some input from a contractor (hopefully not to the point of full, graphed cartoons and all materials) in most examples. At the other extreme, design motifs and weave types conform to the tribal tradition of the makers and hand spun wool and horizontal looms are used.

Village Rugs

There is a long tradition of production at the spontaneous village level in Iran and a selection of the more sought after types is listed with the antique rugs in this book. When trying to assess the present output I have limited the examples to three major groups of carpets and it must be remembered that some of the rugs on the market today would have been made about twenty years ago and may not be produced in the same environment at the moment.

There are fewer of these 'pre Khomeni' pieces around now than were seen five years ago but many can still be found and they represent a unique part of the Iranian carpet output. I spoke with a few dealers, including a large European wholesaler, in an effort to ascertain the exact types and qualities which are currently being produced but received very vague answers to my questions. Part of the reason that this information is elusive seems to be the uncertainty of stockpiles which may still exist within Iran or other countries.

Another portion of this market is made up of carpets which have been used for a number of years, either in Iran or any number of other Western and Asian countries then sold to a dealer who cleans and repairs them before offering them for sale. Some of these rugs are of very good quality and retain the individual charm and tradition of antique items from the area. Most dealers include a selection of these 'middle aged' carpets and they should be examined for signs of chemical washing or fading as well as large repairs or damaged areas.

Hamadan

The city of Hamadan, capital of the province of Kurdistan in western Iran, has a long tradition of carpet distribution and production. The rugs made or sold in the city show a unique weaving style which features a thick cotton weft thread which can be seen clearly from the back of the rug.

Modern rugs of this type are still available and appear in a variety of individual designs and colour schemes which are sometimes named after small towns in the region. Many are no doubt made in the city itself, others in a more isolated environment. All are made with a wool pile tied with a symmetrical knot to a cotton warp and use a thick cotton weft. Some show a fringe on only one end of the carpet, the other warp ends having been flat woven and removed from the loom without being cut.

Detail of Hamadan type weaving showing thick weft thread

Most Hamadan rugs are designed with a geometric medallion of some sort in the central field and quartered sections of the medallion in each corner of the ground which is enclosed by a wide main border with geometric or floral design motifs. The wool is usually of good quality and the colours vary greatly from vibrant reds and blues to more subtle, vegetable dyed tones. Two easily recognised designs are Tuisakhan, which has a very prominent, angular medallion with large 'arrowhead' pendants at each end, and Mazlaghan, which shows a very startling zigzag or serrated-edged medallion with reciprocal patterns around the central field.

Another rug type produced close to this region and known as Karaja, incorporates geometric motifs and large angular or star-shaped medallions drawn in the Caucasian style. Senneh, another town in Kurdistan which is close to the Turkish border, is home to fine kilims and unusual pile rugs which can be recognised by the very rough feel on the back of the rug of the base of the knots. Bidjar is another historical weaving town in the region and the name Kurd is used to describe tribal type rugs from the region which may or may not have a nomadic, tribal origin. Where relevant, these rug types are discussed in the antiques section of the book and any modern production usually conforms to the same design and structural details as old examples, although obviously created in an organised environment.

Shiraz

The city of Shiraz is the capital of Fars province in the south of Iran and lends its name to a large group of rugs which are made by Kashkay (often spelt Qashgai) and Khamseh tribal people who live in the region. The output of these tribes was misnamed after the town of Shiraz during the nineteenth century when the nomads brought their carpets to the town for sale. There has been well organised, although not constant production in the region since the early twentieth century and a number of weaving schools for the revival of traditional crafts have had input into the industry.

Old Shiraz area pile rug, 1.2 × 0.9 m. First half of the 20th century from the Fars province of Iran. Unusual design elements and layout for a rug of this type. Author's collection

Detail of modern Shiraz area pile rug. This small piece shows design and structural details seen in rugs of both Shiraz and Abedah designation. The Persian Carpet Gallery, Adelaide

The Shiraz carpets produced commercially can have a long pile, up to 15 mm, are knotted with an asymmetrical knot to a wool or wool and hair mixed warp and utilise a cotton or wool mix weft. The designs are semi-traditional and include simple geometric flowers, squarish medallions and sometimes small geometric animals or trees, and the most common colours used are red, blue, white, orange and green. They range in size from about 1.4 × 1.2 m to 3 × 2 m, and the knot density, quality and type of wool varies greatly. In most cases the weavings from the Shiraz region are durable and the designs charmingly primitive.

Shiraz is also a major centre for kilims in Iran. Most are slit-woven on a wool or cotton warp and use traditional tribal motifs in a range of abstract designs which are most commonly coloured in bright blues, oranges, reds and whites. The sizes vary from about 2 × 1.2 m to over 3 × 2 m, and most of these flatwoven rugs are hard wearing and practical.

The town of Abedah, to the north of Shiraz, is also a centre of production but most of these pieces are knotted on a cotton warp and the weaving is more regular, designs more tightly drawn and the finished product more perfect in dimension and symmetry than the pieces marketed as Shiraz rugs.

Meshed

The city of Meshed is close to the Afghan border and capital of the province of Khorasan, in north-east Iran. It has been a major marketing centre for carpets made by both nomadic and village dwelling Baluch tribal groups and the descendants of Turkoman people who migrated to the region about eighty years ago. There is also a history of curvilinear designed workshop carpets in the region although I have not seen anything from the source during my research.

Some Baluch rugs from this area are knotted on a cotton warp and it is common to hear a dealer say that this alone is enough to distinguish an Iranian Baluch from its Afghan counterpart, although I do not think that this distinction will remain valid for much longer. Some Baluch type rugs I have seen from this region include a grey cotton weft thread and are of very inferior quality, others are finely knotted on hand spun woollen warp and weft, well designed and subtly coloured and are very durable carpets. The asymmetrical knot is almost always used and knot densities can vary from about 40 to 300 per square inch.

The majority of Turkoman people in the region are descended from Yomud and Tekke subgroups and their weavings are easily recognised by the use of tribal guls as the major field ornament. The ground colour for most of these rugs is red and blue; white or green are used in the designs. They are asymmetrically and symmetrically knotted to densities of up to about 150 per square inch and most pieces use a woollen warp.

Workshop Rugs

Tabriz

The most common rugs from Tabriz are designed with a large central medallion on a plain coloured or sparsely patterned field which includes a semblance of a quartered medallion in each corner and is surrounded by a border of flowers and vines arranged in an 'arabesque' style. It is usual to see symmetrical knots tied to cotton warps, although this cannot always be relied upon when modern workshop production is involved; cotton is also used in the weft. Sometimes, especially in items produced before 1980, the wool has a harsh feel and gives the impression that it will not be very durable. This is, however, not always the case as I have seen Tabriz carpets made with this harsh-feeling wool which appear little used after fifteen years of wear in areas of very heavy traffic.

Large sizes of up to 4 m X almost 3 m can be found and these have a knot density of between 40 and 80 per square inch, the main colour combinations including red, blue and white. If you are interested in Tabriz rugs it is worthwhile searching for a piece that has seen some use on a floor as many dealers carry some in their collections and they can be less expensive than their modern counterparts.

Among the most modern production I viewed were small pieces to about 2 X 1 m which were densely knotted, to a maximum of about 180 per square inch and offered a wide variation of colours.

Nain

Carpets of this designation are usually of wool pile, with areas of silk used to highlight the design, asymmetrically knotted to a cotton warp. The knot density in examples I have seen ranged from about 200 to 400 per square inch and the quality of the wool used in the pile varied from a chemically washed, rather brittle variety to a beautiful, hardwearing fibre which displayed a dull natural sheen that was perfectly complemented by the gleam of white silk flowers.

The most common design shows a central medallion set on a white field which is covered with spandrels and flowers and is enclosed by a main border containing flower head motifs which are connected with vines. Colour combinations containing light and dark blue, white, beige and soft brown are the most common.

Isfahan

Isfahan was the home of Shah Abbas, who sent some of the city's most esteemed artisans to Italy in order to study the decorative arts. During the seventeenth century, when Isfahan was populated by more than 700 000 people and enjoying great prosperity, its looms produced carpets which are thought by many to be among the greatest of the curvilinear designed output of the Persian Empire.

Modern products often use a version of the 'Shah Abbas' border design comprising flowerettes which are interlinked with a simple vine. The range of designs can include a field of animals, birds and flowers, finely detailed in a woollen pile with brightly coloured feathers or petals highlighted in silk, or more classically arranged flowering vines covering a plain coloured ground which contains an intricately decorated medallion. In old pieces the symmetrical knot was almost always used but in modern times the type of knot is not always a reliable guide to geographic origin.

It is my belief that small workshops operate in this region making it possible for more individual products to be made and during my research I found among this rug type some very well made and durable rugs which were well designed and densely knotted. The best pieces seemed to have some age and it was not possible to accurately ascertain how many carpets are produced in the city at the time of writing this book.

I have seen some carpets that appear to have been made in the last thirty years which are very finely knotted—to more than 600 per square inch—and have been inscribed with the name of the designer or master weaver, and his home of Isfahan. These were privately owned and are sought after by collectors of this type of rug.

Qum

The holy city of Qum has given its name to rugs made and or marketed in the area for most of the twentieth century and the weaving characteristics, designs and materials vary. A common type available during the last ten years showed a wool pile, with small areas of silk, asymmetrically knotted to a cotton warp with an average knot density of around 250 per square inch. The carpets have a stiff feel as the weaving is very tight and they are very durable and able to withstand heavy traffic. The designs often show birds and vegetation and the pile is left quite long—to more than 7 mm.

During my most recent excursions into outlets for urban carpets I have not seen any of this type but I did find a variety of all silk pile rug, asymmetrically knotted to a silk warp to

Lounge room furnished with oriental rugs including a large Saltuq.
Courtesy of Mr and Mrs A. Krieg

Modern Qum pile rug, approximately 0.8 × 0.5 m. The Persian Carpet
Gallery, Adelaide

A Kashan pile rug as seen in H. & J. Quigley Antiques, Adelaide

a density of around 500 per square inch, and usually coloured in pink, blue and mauve tones with a more angular design.

Kerman

One of the most easily recognised of the urban rugs of Iran is known by this name. The design almost always includes a long central medallion on a plain coloured, or very sparsely patterned field which is surrounded by a border of flowers. The asymmetrically knotted woollen pile is tied to a cotton warp, usually to a density of no greater than 200 per square inch, and left quite long—to more than 10 mm.

The pile is often made of a soft wool and I was told that during the early 1980s many of the rugs made used Australian wool. The sizes vary from about 1.8 X 1 m to 4 X 3 m or larger and they are seen in a wide variety of colours including red, blue and ivory, and dark blue, pink and mauve combinations. An older piece is probably more desirable as they have a good reputation for durability and are not highly sought after as collector's items and so should be able to be found at a price which compares favourably with items of more recent manufacture.

Kashan

Kashan carpets have a distinctive weaving and design style and, once some have been studied, it should be easy to recognise rugs from this source. The wool pile, asymmetrically knotted to a cotton warp, usually to a density of between 200 and 250 per square inch, is in most cases of good durable quality and the bulk of the output I have viewed appears in medium sizes, often around 2 X 1.3 m.

The most common design shows an elongated, central medallion with quartered segments in each corner of the field which is enclosed by a precisely drawn and intricate border of flowers and vines. There is a wide range of colour combinations available and some of the older pieces on the market show beautiful tones of deep red.

Carpets in larger sizes, different designs, higher knot density and even with a silk pile are occasionally encountered from this source but care should be taken when trying to verify the origin of these pieces. A quality known as Aroon Kashan can also be found and these are usually less densely knotted and less precise in design details although they appear to be made of a durable wool and should be long wearing.

7 Other Carpet Producing Countries

Carpets from Pakistan

A large percentage of the hand-knotted carpets I have viewed while researching this book were made in Pakistan. The products from this country are profuse and relatively inexpensive and so find a place in most showrooms, especially when the display is devoted to only new, mass produced carpets.

As well as the large array of workshop and factory produced goods which are exported from Pakistan there are a few more primitive items that display a tribal background and are made from local, handspun wool. These are more closely related to Afghan weavings than the balance of the Pakistani output and should be named after the tribal group who made them wherever possible.

Tribal Rugs

The Province of Baluchistan, in the west of Pakistan, is a wild and inhospitable area bordering Afghanistan and Iran and stretching to the Persian Gulf in the south. This rugged region is home to nomadic and semi-nomadic Baluch, Pashtun and Pushti tribes as well as other Afghan groups who have traditionally roamed in the area or migrated to the region after the war in Afghanistan began.

The bulk of the products from these tribes are flat-woven, usually in the floating weft technique, using only one or two colours as well as white, black or brown, undyed wool, and are found in small formats. Saddle bags, small storage bags and other household items are more frequently seen than large, floorcovering sizes although some long and thin kilims can be found. Handspun, plied and dyed wool is used and the items appear to have been woven on horizontal looms. Some of the goods of this type which are available could well be up to forty years old and it is difficult to ascertain how much of this kind of weaving is being done now.

Workshop Rugs

The new carpet industry in Pakistan is well organised and most weaving is done by wage earners who work in large workshops or, in the case of smaller business concerns, through subcontract workers who are supplied looms, patterns and materials and are paid when the carpet is completed. The bulk of the output appears in standard designs and knot densities and the practice of washing completed rugs in strong alkaline or acidic solutions is common.

The cheapest and most easily obtained carpets are made in what is known as Princess Bokhara designs, have a knot count of around 180 asymmetrical knots per square inch, a cotton warp and weft and have been very heavily 'washed' in order to make the pile appear lustrous. They are loosely woven, usually in 2.5 × 2 m, 1.8 × 1.2 m or 1.5 × 0.7 m sizes and are seen in a wide variety of colours and a number of versions of the basic pattern, which consists of rows of Turkoman style motifs arranged on a plain field surrounded by multiple borders. In general, these rugs are not durable, not very appealing and mass produced in such large numbers that the major retail dealers are constantly announcing clearance sales or huge price reductions in order to move their stock.

More densely knotted carpets are also made and often these imitate the designs of Iranian rugs. The wool pile in these finer carpets, often having a density of 400 or more asymmetrical knots per square inch, is imported and not so heavily washed in chemicals and these rugs are often hard wearing. All silk or wool with small patches of silk is also seen in the pile of some rugs and I have observed small groups of weavers living in a suburb of Karachi working on wool piled rugs which are knotted with a symmetrical knot to a woollen warp.

There are entrepreneurs who have organised the

Baluch weaving, 2.5 × 0.3 m. Second half of the 20th century from the region around Quetta, Baluchistan province, Pakistan. Finely woven, floating weft brocade used as a decorative strip and adorned with shells. Author's collection

Details of the decorative weaving above

A typical Pakistani 'Bokhara', approximately 1.2 × 0.8 m. The Persian Carpet Gallery, Adelaide

Baluch bag, 0.5 × 0.5 m. Second half of the 20th century, Baluchistan/Iran border regions. The piece was originally a quorjin but had been cut before being sold as a single bag. Floating weft brocade face, plainweave back. Author's collection

production of imitation Iranian rugs—reproducing similar size, design, colour and quality ranges as well as imitating the weaving style and knotting detail of various centres in Iran. It is almost impossible to organise the output of the country into groups based on the geographical location of manufacture as identical rugs may be made in more than one workshop, town or city.

The produce of smaller workshops seems to be of better quality than the more commercially available 'Pakistani Bokharas' and a good general rule would be to look for rugs which are densely packed rather than considering the loosely woven items, even if the latter are said to contain more knots per square inch and especially if the pile looks unnaturally shiny.

Carpets from India and Nepal

Hand made carpets are produced in many parts of India. The asymmetrical knot is used in almost all of them and most rugs are made with a woollen pile and a cotton warp and weft. A variety of designs is made including many curvilinear, central medallion rugs with flowers and vines, large trees containing multi-coloured birds and surrounded by animals, and geometric shapes which are reminiscent of Caucasian motifs.

All are produced within a well organised environment and, even though there is a large 'cottage industry' supplying this market, I have classified them in this book as workshop carpets.

Workshop Carpets

The most densely knotted carpets come from Kashmir, in the north, and both silk and wool piles are knotted to a cotton warp to densities varying from around 200 to 500 per square inch. There is a wide range of colours and designs and an occasional rug which has a silk pile knotted to silk warps is seen. I have been told by Indian manufacturers that the use of Chinese silk is common as it is cheaper than the local product.

A variety of other items are woven in Kashmir and these include chainstitched embroideries which are produced in small carpet sizes and are usually on an all woollen plain weave with trees, animals, birds, flowers and the occasional central medallion, hand-embroidered to the ground, and a number of finely woven, woollen scarves or shawls which are produced in a variety of embroidery techniques. At the time of writing this book, Kashmir was at war with the Indian government in a fight for an autonomous country and it is not known whether this will greatly affect the output for a prolonged period of time.

Wool piled rugs knotted on cotton warps to densities of between about 160 and 280 per square inch are made in many other areas of India including the Punjab, the east of

Detail of a typical wool pile with silk inlay rug from Kashmir. John Hall

Typical small rug from Uttar Pradesh, 1.0 × 0.6 m. Donovan Winch

Woman knotting rug in Nepal, 1989

neighbouring country of Nepal are ethnic Tibetan people who have been living in exile from their country, many for more than forty years. Tibetan settlements can be found all over the subcontinent in cities and rural areas including Delhi, Madras, Darjeeling and in Patan, a suburb of Kathmandu. The people live in a close, communal environment and wool is bulk-purchased, handspun (usually on a spinning wheel) and dyed by a resident dye-master, then knotted on a vertical loom to a cotton warp, to densities of between 40 and 80 per square inch and using the 'Tibetan knot' as described in Chapter 1.

Design motifs are knotted from graphed cartoons and a bulk buyer can choose from either vegetable or chemical dyed wool and create individual rugs by arranging the central field and borders with whatever mix of individual motifs is desired.

The products of these small workshops are usually very durable and most of the dyes are properly fixed. The edges of patterns have a sculptured appearance as they are trimmed a little lower than the surrounding area when the pile is cut and a mixture of Chinese type design motifs, mythical Tibetan animals and more contemporary patterns is found.

Detail of a typical Chinese rug. Donovan Winch

Rajahstan and Uttar Pradesh. The coarsest quality of Indian rug is made from a wool or sometimes wool and jute mixed pile asymmetrically knotted to densities between 30 and 80 per square inch, to a cotton or jute warp. These include Chinese type designs as well as the familiar floral medallion and plain coloured rugs. Many of these pieces are made in the home but a graphed pattern and all materials are supplied to the weavers and they are more suited to a workshop definition as designs, knot qualities and sizes can be bulk ordered.

There is also a flat-woven rug made in India which is known as a durrie. These usually use the double interlocking technique and are made from a variety of materials including cotton wefts on cotton warps, cotton wefts on jute warps, wool wefts on cotton warp and a variety of wool/jute combinations. The least expensive types that I have seen cannot be washed without the dyes running profusely but much of the other output is of a good, durable quality and often available through large Western retail stores.

Another group of weavers working in India and the

Typical Russian rug from the Caucasus region. M. and G. Drummond

Carpets from Other Centres

Hand-knotted and woven oriental carpets are and have been made in many other countries of the world including Yugoslavia, Roumania, Morocco, Bangladesh and some Southeast Asian countries, but I have seen little of the output from these centres in the outlets I have visited although access to manufacturers can be obtained through international trade journals. The only substantial groups of carpets which remain to be mentioned are made in a workshop environment in the USSR and China.

China

Chinese carpets can be found in a wide size, design and colour range and almost always use the asymmetrical knot in densities of between 60 and 160 per square inch. Most have a long (to 15 mm or more) woollen pile which is 'embossed' in the manner of the Tibetan refugee output and use a cotton warp and weft. Silk carpets are also made and some of these are more finely knotted; some can also be found with a silk pile and silk warps and wefts.

Most of the woollen piled rugs have been lightly washed but are still very durable and are produced in such large size and colour ranges that they find their way into a wide variety of retail outlets. The most inexpensive Chinese woollen piled rug is not hand knotted but described as hand hooked. These pieces have a woven base to which the pile is hooked rather than tied. They are usually backed with hessian and can be easily recognised as the base of the pile knots cannot be seen on the back of the rug.

The USSR

There has been a variety of rug types produced in the USSR. Many incorporate design motifs which are traditional to the geographic origin or ethnic background of the maker, but the workshops in which they are made do not provide a good environment for individuality and most examples I have viewed have a familiar, mass-produced feel about them.

The major styles include those made in the manner of Turkoman carpets, with a woollen pile, asymmetrically knotted to a woollen warp and weft. Most I have seen have been in small sizes, not greater than 2 X 1.4 m and the wool used has been durable and naturally lustrous. They are densely knotted and hard wearing but the Turkoman design guls are often too cluttered on the field and seem crowded by multiple borders.

Other woollen pile carpets, asymmetrically knotted to cotton warps, are made in the east of Soviet Central Asia and are called Samarkands. They use Chinese influenced design motifs as well as motifs from old rugs from the region. A wide range of colour schemes can be found in a variety of sizes.

The last major group of Russian rugs I have seen are produced in the Caucasus Mountains. They are named after the town whose historical design motifs are used or by the name of the area where the rugs were made. They have a woollen pile, symmetrically knotted to a cotton base, and are most often seen with large, geometric, star-shaped medallions, referred to when seen in antique rugs as the Leshgi Star, placed on a plain ground and surrounded by borders of serrated leaf and wine glass motifs. They are usually chemically washed and a wide range of colours can be found. The most common sizes are small rugs or long hallway runners.

Most rugs that I have viewed which were made in the USSR appear very durable and there is a variety of design styles to choose from.

Heriz pile rug, 1.9 ✗ 1.54 m. Second half of the 19th century. Nomadic Rug Traders

ANTIQUE ORIENTAL CARPETS

The term 'antique' can be ambiguous and it is necessary to examine some of the implied meanings before focusing on any particular rug type. In my experience I have been affected by specific interpretations of the word when importing carpets into Australia as the official rule regarding non-payment of duty on antique goods states an age of more than one hundred years. Other organisations governing the ethics of antique dealers have used a more variable index to quantify the 'antique' value of an item and have placed the age of an antique oriental rug at more than sixty years.

When writing articles for specialist antique magazines I have researched a wide range of items and discovered many which were less than one hundred years old yet deserved the title of antique as they were made in a unique manner or by a unique group of people whose living environment has completely disappeared. I have also seen a number of examples of products which are over a hundred years old but appear to have little ethnographic merit or intrinsic, collectable value.

Among oriental rugs there are similar inconsistencies and I have chosen to include only examples which conform to my own personal interpretation of 'antique'. This relates to the manner in which the rugs were created and the way of life of the makers as much as a carpet's age. At the same time, I believe there should be some limit on the age of a piece and I have not included any examples which were made after the first quarter of the twentieth century—a period of great change for the majority of primitive people living in rug producing countries.

For examples of specific carpet types I have used rugs from the collections of private individuals, major Australian dealers and my own supplies. Most have been imported into Australia over the last ten years from Afghanistan, Turkey, Pakistan, the UK, Europe and the USA.

As there are restrictions on the number of carpet types which can be included in this book I have focused mainly on tribal and village weavings and this is a statement on my own personal tastes and my individual judgement of intrinsic 'antique' value. Some of the workshop sources listed were, until the mid nineteenth century, centres of a village weaving tradition, but major western and local commercial interests greatly influenced the production after this time and the examples discussed are from this later output.

A decision was also made about the rugs included in this section on the basis of availability to my readers so that the information and colour plates could be used when making comparative judgements on carpets they viewed. It seemed pointless to me to arrange a group of antique items which were totally out of reach to the bulk of the public and would have more relevance as a museum catalogue than an instructional guide to assessing carpets on the market.

8 Antique Tribal Carpets

Turkoman

The Turkoman are one of the major tribal groups whose nineteenth century handicrafts are available on the retail market. Many pieces from the turn of the century retain their tribal integrity and those made before about 1880 offer the collector an opportunity to preserve a unique portion of the tribes' heritage. The output of the Turkoman tribes is usually divided into subtribal groups and I have included three major categories in this section.

Almost all of the large carpets made are designed in rows of traditional, geometric tribal motifs or guls. The border motifs and minor guls which appear in the field also help to distinguish the age and identity of the tribal maker and there are many consistencies of weave type and pile knot used among the individual groups. One type of carpet that is unique to the Turkoman groups is known as an Engsi or a Hatchli. These rugs, usually no bigger than 2 × 1.5 m, were used to hang in the doorway of a tent and are designed with a large cross which quarters the field and has a skirt of motifs along the bottom edge which can take the form of trees, flowers or small diamond shapes.

The Turkomans are also known for their smaller weavings which include a range of storage bags named after their size ranging from Mafresh, the smallest, usually about 0.7 × 0.3 m, to Juval, which can be as large as 1.4 × 0.8 m. Some flatwoven items were also produced and these include storage bags and floor rugs.

Carpets were produced in nomadic and semi-nomadic environments and, on occasion, some extra large pieces were made on order for a specific khan or local leader, but all were made within the tribal environment and display the design motifs, weaving style and materials which are typical of individual subgroups.

A major marketing point for Turkoman rugs during the 19th century was the city of Bukhara in west Turkestan, and dealers from the time named the rugs after that city. When looking at antique rugs today it is a good general rule to stay clear of anyone who markets a rug by this name unless you are sure of assessing its origin and age yourself as most reputable dealers try to label a rug by the most specific terms available and it is much more common to find a genuine piece named by the overall or sub-tribal group. It should be noted, however, that many antique dealers who do not specialise in carpets, especially those who have done business in England over a long period of time, still use the term Bukhara and often have some good items in their collections.

Ersari

One of the largest subgroups to survive the Russian intervention at the beginning of this century, the Ersari ranged from Turkestan to the northern regions of Afghanistan. When the tribal living structure was being replaced by a more ordered and organised environment many Ersari clans migrated further south, into Afghanistan and away from the newly formed Soviet states. The descendants of these Turkoman tribes still exist in the north of Afghanistan today.

Ersari carpets are knotted, with an asymmetrical knot, on a woollen warp and weft, to a maximum density of around 80 per square inch. The main field ornament is known as a 'Gulli' gul and is large in size, of almost square proportions, and arranged in usually two or three rows of no more than four guls each. In some pieces the corners of the eight sided gul are indented, giving the square shape a roundish appearance.

Even in large carpets the guls are spaced evenly and do not usually appear crowded. A common motif in the minor borders is the small, linked 'boteh' and colours range from

Turkoman Juval, circa 1900, 1.2 × 0.8 m. Extra weft wrapped front and plain weave back in this traditional storage bag made by an Ersari group from Afghan Turkestan. Author's collection

Turkestan and many rugs were made by tribal people while and after the Trans-Caspian states were being established. Some groups also escaped to Iran and settled in the region around Meshed where they were later joined by Yomud people. These groups continued to make carpets, but by the 1930s the original style, colours and design motifs usually bore little resemblance to their early work.

The main design motif is known as the Tekke gul which is small in size, usually no bigger than 20 × 15 cm, and placed on the field at the intersections of thin, dark lines which divide the whole ground. The gul is quartered by these lines and often contains geometric flower type motifs and other ornamentation which always has a very formal feel. In between these major guls are ram's horn-ended minor motifs, of a basic cross shape with diagonal or latch-hooked embellishments. Small, very angular and basic wine glass motifs or geometric forms with ram's horn ends are often found in the borders and a range of madder red and copper tones, beautiful indigo blues, mauves, bright cochineal red and white are used.

In large carpets, to about 3 × 2.5 m, there are not usually more than five rows of ten to twelve major guls and the ground colour in most pieces made in Turkestan up to about 1910 is more likely to have a bronze or brownish tone than red. Pieces made before about 1870 are not often larger than 2.6 × 2.3 m, including the long kilim ends which are another aid to identification.

Hatchlis were also made and these usually had chocolate brown coloured skirts which contained small diamond shapes and utilised a large, basic tree type design in the main borders. At the top of the cross shape in the main field a small triangular mihrab is usually found. A range of piled bags and household decorations including camel trappings and doorway surrounds were also made and these often display the finest weaving skills.

An asymmetrical knot on a wool warp with a wool weft

beautiful madder red, green, blue and sometimes yellow to more monotoned arrangements of dark madder red/brown, blue and small amounts of white.

Most Ersari carpets are seen in larger formats and range in size from about 2 × 3 m to 3 × 6 m. Some prayer rugs can be found and these usually have the ram's horn motif atop the geometric mihrab. Hatchlis, and kilims can also be found as well as a selection of storage bags. The most common type of kilim is woven on a wool warp and utilises an extra weft brocade technique to produce smallish diamond shaped motifs which cover the main field. Many of these pieces are seen in dark red, blue, black and small amounts of white.

Tekke

The Tekke tribe was one of the most powerful of the Turkoman groups at the time of Russia's re-organisation of

Room in an Adelaide house showing a Tekke Hatchli (centre wall), some antique Turkish weavings and other oriental rugs

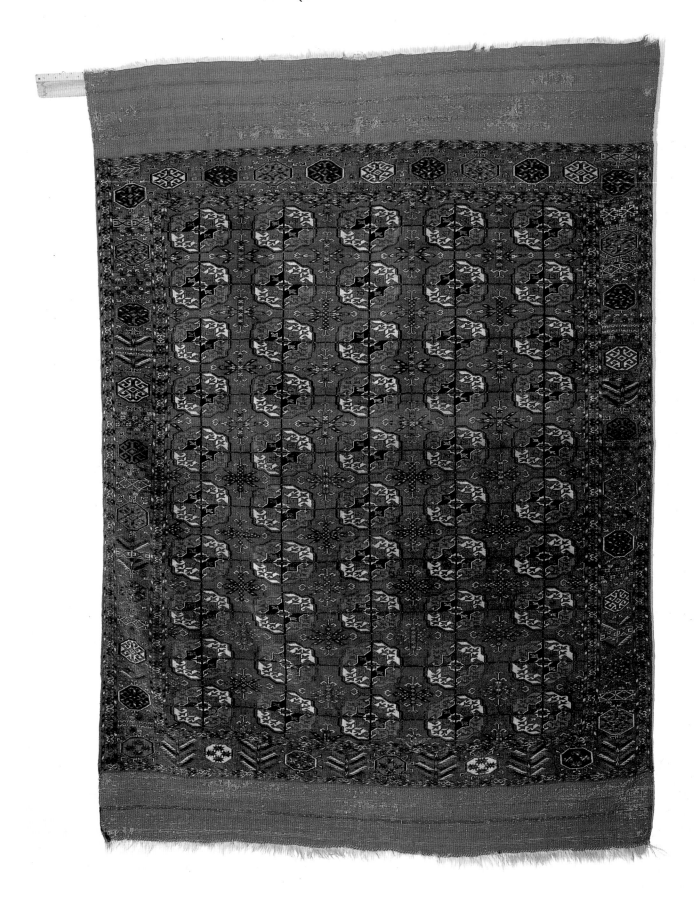

Opposite page: *Tekke main carpet. Area of pile 2.1 X 2.2 m. Second half of the 19th century.* Nomadic Rug Traders

Yomud pile rug, circa 1900, 2.6 X 1.5 m. The Kepse gul is used in this rug from Turkestan. The Lindley Collection

was almost always used and densities varied from about 120 per square inch to over 500 in some of the finest Juvals and Kapunuk (a weaving to decorate the tent opening). It is usual for the larger pieces to be less finely woven than smaller items but floor rugs of about 1.8 X 1.2 m can sometimes be found which are very densely knotted. In most cases the warp threads are all on the same level but occasionally one side of the knots is indented and this causes alternate warps to be depressed.

In later pieces from Turkestan, aniline dyes which faded dramatically were used, but up until about 1920 the weaving style, materials, design motifs and layout is still typical of Tekke carpets even though the early balance of design is usually lost and the colours have sometimes faded to about ten per cent of their original clarity. The rugs made in Iran were by this time using a range of motifs which had evolved from a mixture of Yomud and Tekke traditions. These carpets are most often seen with a red ground and blue and white ornaments and both the asymmetrical and symmetrical knot were used. The weaving style has continued in the region until modern times and there are few pieces around that can be convincingly dated as turn of the century goods.

Yomud

Yomud weavers used one of the widest colour selections of any Turkoman group and rugs containing white, yellow, a wide range of blue, blue/green and turquoise tones and many red, copper, brown and mauve shades can be found. Three major guls were used and the ground colour of the main border, which often contained an angular flower motif or linked geometric shape and was enclosed by a small 'running dog' border, was usually white. The sophisticated Kepse gul is broadly diamond shaped but is made up of small vertical compartments surrounding a squared central shape. These compartments alternate in colour and contain a hooked geometric motif. The guls are evenly spaced on a plain coloured field and early pieces have a beautiful balance which makes the guls appear to float on the field.

Yomud juval, late 19th century. Steve Wallace

The Yomud gul is more formal with square ends and angular sides and is usually used in conjunction with a minor gul and the Dynak gul appears as a diamond with hooked shapes, similar to the running dog, attached to each side on a plain ground.

Both the asymmetrical and symmetrical knots on woollen warps and woollen wefts are seen although most are found with a symmetrical knot. The density varies from about 80 to 400 per square inch, the most finely knotted items being small bags and household items. Hatchlis appear in a variety of design styles, and a household weaving called an Asmalyk (which has one triangular shaped side, is usually about 1.2 X 0.6 m in size and was used as a decoration for the bridal camel) can also be found.

Baluch

The Baluch tribal groups roamed over an area that stretched from the borders of Turkestan in the north to the shores of the Arabian Sea in the south and from central Iran to the

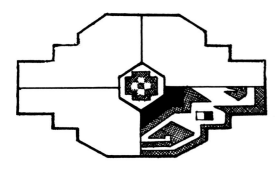

One quarter of a Yomud gul

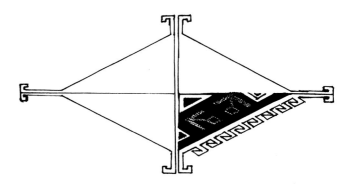

One quarter of a Dynak gul

Collection of Yomud piled trappings showing: an Asmalyk, a Mafresh measuring 0.4 ×
0.7 m, and an Okbash, which W. Loges says were used to cover the ends of tent poles,
the piled area of which measures 0.28 × 0.6 m. Nomadic Rug Traders

borders of Sind Province of Pakistan. The tribal structure is complicated and there are many subtribes which show individual styles and designs even though they have much in common with the broader category. Carpets can be found in a wide variety of sizes from about 4 × 3 m to small prayer rugs of less than 1 × 1.2 m and a number of household accoutrements are seen including pile front saddle bags, known as quorjin, and other storage bags, floating weft brocade small bags used to carry horse shoes, the Koran or as vanity bags for storage of personal hygiene items.

Kilims are usually seen woven in the floating weft brocade technique and range in size from small sofre, special eating mats, and ru-kursi, used to cover the knees of a small group of people and a small charcoal brazier which was placed in the middle to keep the freezing cold of the night at bay, to large floor coverings of about 4 × 2 m. It is common to find kilims which have been woven in two pieces about one metre wide then joined together after the weaving process is completed. This was presumably done because the tribal weavers found it difficult to construct a wide loom and so made the desired rug in two halves.

Because of the huge range of products which are sometimes described by a sub-tribal name and at other times can only be distinguished by the region in which the tribe

Baluch Quorjin, circa 1900. Author's collection

Detail of Baluch Ru-Kursi or Sofre, circa 1920. Mixed technique utilising plainweave, slitwoven tapestry, knotted pile and floating weft brocade. Private collection, Adelaide

Detail of Baluch kilim, circa 1920. Floating weft brocade and plain weave from Afghanistan. Author's collection

Adelaide solicitor's office showing antique Baluch carpet

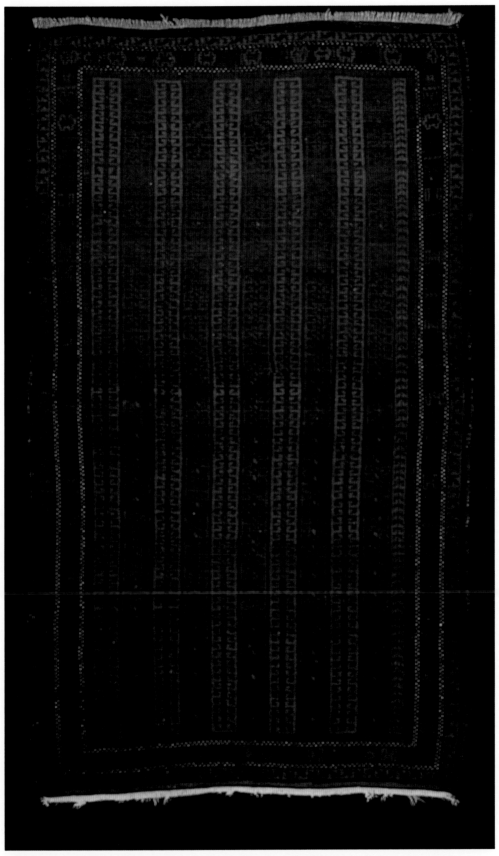

Baluch pile rug, circa 1920, 2.4 × 1.4 m. Iran/Afghan border region. An example of the 'Black' Baluch type. Private collection, Adelaide

Baluch pile rug, circa 1920, Afghanistan. An example of the 'Black' Baluch type,
probably from the Mushwanee subtribe. Private collection, Adelaide

roamed, it is difficult to offer any identifying characteristics which apply to all Baluch rugs except that they are nearly always knotted, in most cases with a symmetrical knot, to woollen warps and use woollen wefts. Camel hair is sometimes used in areas of the pile and goat or horse hair is also found in the base weave of Baluch rugs.

Even among prayer rugs there is a wide variation in design motifs, layout and colours used and many distinctly separate groups can be seen. The rugs from Turkestan are usually asymmetrically knotted on a woollen warp and weft to a density of around 100 per square inch and sometimes contain camel hair in areas of the pile. It is common to see long, flatwoven end treatments which employ very fine slitweaving, floating weft brocade and plain weave in alternating stripes to a length of a sometimes 20 cm, and the mihrab in most prayer rugs is of square proportions, often containing a central tree motif. The major colours seen are brown, a number of red and blue tones, some yellow and an occasional green or olive shade.

Some of the most colourful Baluch rugs were made by a group that is known as Kurd/Baluch and it has been suggested that this group migrated or was forcibly relocated to the Khorasan Province of Iran from the Turkish/Iran border regions and was once a Kurdish tribe. Many of the design motifs used can be found in the rugs made by Anatolian Kurds and it is common to see the tarantula motif and the magic S shape as a minor border motif. The colours include a range of red and blue tones including a clear blue/green, natural white and ivory and some pink or purplish tones. The symmetrical knot is used to a density of no more than about 80 per square inch and the warp and weft material is wool. It is common to see natural camel hair used in the pile.

Other Baluch rugs from the Khorasan province were often finely knotted, to about 150 asymmetrical knots per square inch on a wool warp, and used a wool weft. Prayer rugs usually contained an angular or square shaped mihrab which surrounded a large tree motif on a camel hair ground. Other examples show a well balanced, angular flower and vine border which surrounded a field of triangular flower motifs. The colours used were mostly darkish reds, blues, mauves and natural brown, white or ivory wool or camel hair. Kilims were also made in the floating weft brocade technique and these contained mostly dark colours.

The products of some subtribal groups can be fairly easily recognised and these include the Jacob Khani, which usually use only madder red tones, a black colour that is often corroded and sometimes greyish colours and very small areas of white. The main ornament takes the form of a large, narrow, elongated diamond which is repeated on the field and has latchhooks or arrow shapes attached to its side giving it the look of a candelabra. The border usually contains a very angular flower and vine design.

Another large group of rugs contain only very dark tones of blue, black, deep madder red and mauve tinged, dark

wool. The pile is lustrous and the design elements can vary but the subtle mix of deep tones is easily recognised. These rugs are collectively known as 'Black Baluch' and I believe that they come from a variety of individual clans and from a wide geographical area, the centre of which is the Iran/Afghan border regions from the Seistan desert to the Meshed region, in the north. The main subtribe who are mentioned in connection with this type of weaving are the Mushwanee.

Some antique Baluch rugs were made in an organised setting from as early as the 1870s and it is difficult to tell what the environment in which they were created was like, but most were made originally to supply a local market and have a tribal integrity. The town of Seistan, in Iran, was one such centre and many prayer rugs were produced there. They usually contain roundish, architectural shapes in the mihrab which appear to represent the dome of a mosque, are asymmetrically knotted to a woollen warp to a density of up to about 120 knots per square inch and use a wool, or sometimes cotton weft. The colours include yellow, a range of red and blue tones, white, dark browns, and sometimes black which has corroded.

Baluch carpets, especially small items like quorjin and prayer rugs, are a perfect place for the new collector to begin as they are still inexpensive in comparison to other items from a similar background or of comparative age, as well as offering a wide range of styles. Baluch kilims from Afghanistan, Baluchistan province of Pakistan and the Iranian border regions, which are woven in two sections by the floating weft brocade technique, can also be found and these display the unique skill and delicacy of design of the best tribal weavings, yet have so far been largely ignored by Western markets. Even large pile carpets of obvious nomadic manufacture from the 1920s and 30s are seen in good condition and are valued at far less than a similar sized new item from a well marketed centre.

Kashkay

The Kashkay was a confederacy of tribes which lived in the Fars province of south Iran for at least three hundred years. Their traditional lifestyle involved a twice yearly trek from the plains on the lowlands which stretched to the Persian Gulf to the Zagros Mountains, in the north of the province, following the grass which was needed for the survival of their livestock. Reports on the number of tribes in the confederacy vary depending on the time of research, but there have been up to fifty individual clans at some stages in their history.

In 1956 the Iranian government officially disbanded the confederacy and by 1972 when the Department of Tribal Education, which has been responsible for imposing an institutional structure onto these essentially nomadic graziers, estimated that the number of Kashkay people was

Kashkay kilim, 2.4 X 1.5 m. Second half of the 19th century. Nomadic Rug Traders

Khamseh pile rug, 2.55 X 1.6 m. 19th century. Nomadic Rug Traders

Kashkay Quorjin, circa 1900. Photographed as it would have been made. P. and M. MacNamara

Luri pile rug, 4.2 X 1.75 m. Late 19th century from west Iran. John Leach Tribal Rug and Kilim Gallery

about 140 000, of which about two thirds were still trying to live a nomadic existence, only six distinct groups could be recognised.

When viewing the rugs of the Kashkay tribes several types of weaving styles can be seen and both the asymmetrical and the symmetrical knot are used in piled items. Warp and weft threads are of wool, wool and goat hair mix or goat hair, and most rugs are designed around one or more diamond shaped medallions, usually latchhooked, and contain an array of flower and often animal motifs which are geometric in form although all the edges are softened. Some dealers will attempt classification of the specific subgroup who produced the piece, others will refer to major design elements as a way of distinguishing between rug types. It is not of great concern how they are grouped inside the broader category as most research into the origins of tribal rugs involves speculation and is an evolving process. As new specialist books are published, new labels for describing rug types are used and the keen collector, once embarked on his or her chosen path, will keep up to date with reading material and form an opinion based on personal experience and individual research.

Pieces from the third quarter of the nineteenth century are rare and valuable and represent a unique portion of the tribal rugs available to collectors. They are elegant in design, utilise a wide variety of vegetable dyes and are found in sizes to about 2.5 X 1.5 m. Pieces made as late as the turn of the century can contain only vegetable dyed wool and are worthy of collection.

Kilims were usually made in the slitwoven tapestry method and the colours used included a range of clear blue, green and red tones, white and the occasional yellow. They often appear in bold designs with large diamond shaped medallions with an array of geometric flower motifs scattered on a plain coloured field and surrounded by two narrow borders of small, stepped shapes. It is usual to find a single or double row of weft brocade along each end of the kilim and these are often of just blue and white colours. A range of quorjin can also be found and many collectors prefer these smaller items as it enables them to obtain more pieces and avoid storage and display problems.

Khamsah

The Khamsah were another south Persian confederacy which contained five major tribes. These included two of Arabic origin and the Farsi speaking Basseri. Their carpets are similar in appearance to those of the Kashkay although the Arab groups almost always include the chicken motif in the design. This motif varies from an almost indistinguishable angular bird shaped object which is an integral part of a larger medallion to distinct, geometric chickens which are scattered on the field. The major colours used are a variety of red and blue tones, white and brown. Both the asymmetrical and the symmetrical knot are used and wool, wool and hair mix or goat hair are used in the base weave. A variety of quorjin and bags can also be found.

Luri

Luri groups are found in Fars Province, in the Veramin area of North Iran and in Luristan province in the west of Iran. Their weavings are found in a variety of formats including pile rugs, kilims, quorjin, horse blankets, and small bags. The saddlebags from the west and north of Iran often include soumak weaving and knotted pile and are usually large, each bag being about 1 × 0.7 m. Pile rugs often have a single thick overcast cord used as selvedge and usually are made of a lustrous wool. Almost all weavings utilise wool or wool and hair mixed warps and a variety of design motifs can be found.

The kilims from Fars are likely to be less densely patterned than Kashkay weavings although most appear in the large diamond medallion format. It is also possible to find a variety of weaving techniques in the same piece, including soumak and knotted pile highlights on a plainweave ground. This often occurs in household items like bags and horse or camel trappings.

Bakhtiar

The carpets and weavings of the Bakhtiari tribe can be divided into two main groups. The tribe itself is related to the Luri and a major portion of weavings named after the tribe were made in the province of Luristan. These use a variety of design motifs including angular floral shapes, geometric animals and, sometimes, a version of the swastika motif is seen in the borders. Most of this output appears in flat-woven covers and quorjin which utilise plain weave, soumak and knotted pile borders or end panels and it is common to find large saddlebags labelled Luri/Bakhtiar as it can be very difficult to distinguish between some items.

Pile carpets made in this region and further north in Kurdistan Province often utilise compartmented, in either square or diamond format, fields which contain trees and flowers and are symmetrically knotted to a cotton warp with a thick cotton weft, in the style of Hamadan carpets. These are not usually older than about 1910 and are probably more suited to a village classification but have retained their tribal description in order to distinguish them from other traditional village centres and because they were made by settled members of the tribe.

The majority of Bakhtiari carpets were produced in villages in the Chahar Mahal region, west of Isfahan, by large groups of Bakhtiari tribespeople who began settling in the region around the turn of the century. The tribe traditionally was semi-nomadic, making a yearly migration to the mountains in search of pasture for their flocks. There were very powerful khans who controlled subgroups and by 1910 these leaders had organised a number of small workshop enterprises in the region to provide carpets for their homes. Many of these are inscribed and very finely knotted and seem to me to be strongly out of place among tribal carpets, yet must be included in the category.

Most of the Chahar Mahal Bakhtiari carpets utilise the compartmented field design or a floral, central medallion and are knotted to a cotton warp and weft to an average density of about 150 per square inch. They appear in sizes ranging from 1.8 × 1.2 m to about 3 × 2 m and are not usually older than the turn of the century. Some earlier, obviously nomadic tribal weavings can be found and these include quorjin and other small pile work and flat weaving. All of these use a symmetrical knot and woollen base weave. A beautiful Bakhtiar carpet appears on the frontispiece (page 2).

Afshar

Most rugs known as Afshar come from the Kirman province of southwest Iran. They are often knotted, with one side of the knot indented, causing alternate warps to be partially depressed, on a woollen base and it is common to see the use of a red weft. Many appear in small sizes from about 1 × 1 m to 1.8 × 1.2 m and some are designed with large boteh shapes covering the field. In other examples the field is of squarish proportion with triple, triangular end decorations and smaller medallions of the same shape on

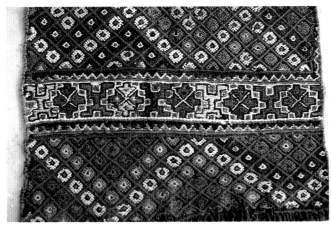

Top: *Luri or Bakhtiar kilim, circa 1900, 2.6 × 0.7 m. Cicim embroidery and weft wrapped end borders from the west of Iran. Probably a baggage wrap.* Author's collection

Above: *Detail of top picture*

Right: *Bakhtiar pile rug, 1.95 × 1.4 m. Early 20th century from the west of Iran.* P. and P. Appelbee

a plain ground. The most common colours used are red, blue and white and examples can be found which originate from as far north as Azerbaijan.

In pieces from the Kerman area which were made after the early twentieth century the warp threads are almost always cotton and the pile knot is deeply indented on one side. Some flatwoven items are found including weft-wrapped kilims with geometric animal and flower shapes and small bags. Knotted pile quorjin or quorjin fronts can also be seen and these often provide the best surviving examples of their work.

Shahsavan

The name Shahsavan was first seen around the turn of the sixteenth century during the reign of Shah Ismail whose family originated in the Azerbaijan province of Iran. The weavings which are given this name are usually Soumak woven kilims, bags or horse blankets and are commonly designed with angular medallions, diamond shaped motifs and geometric animal or human forms. Pile rugs can also be found but many of these are named after the geographic region rather than the tribal group, as it is difficult to justify a Shahsavan origin even when design motifs, materials and weaving are typical. Most common colours found include bright red, orange, pink, purple and a variety of blue tones and the white portions of the design elements were sometimes made of cotton.

The Shahsavan are of Turkic origin and the influence of other Turkic tribes, like the Afshar, Armenian and Kurdish groups, as well as the many individual khanates established in the southern Caucasus Mountains where a unique and individual weaving style had evolved, can be discerned in rugs named after the tribe. Jenny Housego, who did considerable fieldwork in the Azerbaijan province of Iran during the 1970s, has published some of her findings and divided the weavings into subtribal groupings which included geographical notations as well as individual clans like the Baghadi and the Inanlu.

It must also be remembered that the Azerbaijan region extended into parts of present day Turkey, the USSR and Iran and it has always been common for rug types to be named after a trading centre. Shahsavan weavings may have been called after their Caucasian, Turkish or Iranian counterparts before sufficient research had been done. There is also the possibility that unrelated weavings are attributed to the Shahsavan but should be named after their geographic origin or separate tribal group. These uncertainties are part of the appeal of traditional oriental rugs and the Shahsavan of Azerbaijan are fascinating for the collector to study.

Kurds

There are three major Kurdish rug groups which can be found. It is easiest to classify these by the geographic region of production as the specific groups show individual weaving and design styles. From the north-east of Iran, in Khorashan province, comes a group of rugs which are often called Quchan Kurds, after a town in the region. The piled pieces often utilise very basic Turkoman guls or geometric motifs and a wide colour range can be found. They are symmetrically knotted on a wool or, especially in pieces made after 1920, cotton warp to a density which is usually no greater than 50 per square inch. Some kilims are found and many of these are in the form of mixed technique sofre, eating mats. A combination of plain weave and weft wrapping is the usual format for these long and thin or square shaped items and it is common to see a small amount of asymmetrically knotted pile in the design highlights. The most common colour combinations include a salmon pink, soft brown, white and sky blue. Quorjin can also be found and the most common design format is an all over hooked diamond pattern surrounded by a narrow border which often contains a reciprocal ram's horn motif.

Kurdish pile rugs are also made in the west of Iran and

are sometimes known as Varamin Kurds. They usually have a symmetrically knotted woollen pile and a woollen base weave and are not usually denser than 70 per square inch. The piled front quorjin from this group are sometimes more finely knotted and display the largest range of colours. The main design element in all pieces is a hooked diamond motif which covers the field and the colours include a range of blue tones, red, a soft pink, dark brown, white and the occasional yellow. The wool in the pile of most nineteenth century pieces is lustrous and they are durable and beautiful rugs.

Kilims from this region utilise a variety of design motifs but it is common to see some extra weft wrapping around the edges of the slit-woven design in the manner of the diamond motif kilims which were made by the Kurdish tribes around Van, in present day Turkey.

The third major group of Kurdish rugs come from Turkey and are usually described by the region in which they were made or marketed. Van is one of the centres which is often mentioned and most of the output from the region is in the form of slitwoven kilims, often made of two complementary halves which are joined together after the weaving process is completed. The design was nearly always made up of rows of diamond motifs and a wide range of red, blue, blue/green and ivory tones can be found.

Another centre is Malattya and both kilims and pile rugs have been attributed to the town. The colours are usually deep blues, blue/green tones, madder red and bronze tones and white, and in pile rugs the major design elements are small tarantula motifs, large, double diamond shapes and small S signs scattered in the field. Piled prayer rugs can be found and the most finely knotted of the Yoruk Kurds

Kurdish knotted pile bag face. Late 19th century from the west of Iran. M. and A. Thompson

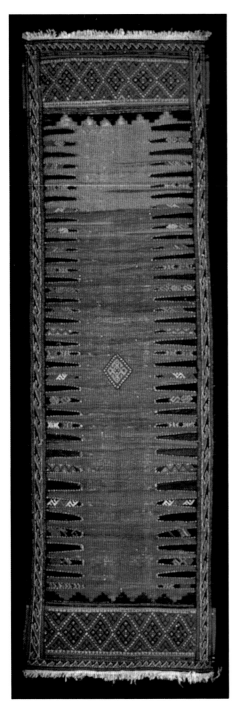

Kurdish Sofre, circa 1920, 2.7 × 0.7 m.
Plain weave and cicim embroidery from
the Khorasan province of Iran. Private
collection, Adelaide

Kurd/Yoruk prayer rug, circa 1890, 1.6 × 1.1 m. Malattya region, eastern
Turkey. Author's collection

(a word that is used in Turkey to mean nomad) are said to come from this region. They are always symmetrically knotted to a density of around 160 per square inch in the finest examples, on a woollen warp and often have a red dyed weft.

Other prayer rugs and longer format, to 2.5 × 1.4 m, pile rugs with similar design motifs are also known as Yoruk rugs or are named after different geographical regions. The other major centres and recognisable rug groups include Gaziantep, Urfa and Hakkari, in the south-east of Turkey.

Uzbek kilim, circa 1890, 3.8 X 1.8 m. Double interlocking tapestry from Turkestan.
Author's collection

Yuncu

A group of weavings can be found which were made in the west of Turkey, in the Balikiser region, by a nomadic tribal group called the Yuncu, which is translated to mean wool merchant, and these are usually slitwoven kilims or saddlebags which display bold 'centipede' motifs in the main field, often including a version of the 'tarantula' and showing star shaped designs in the border. The main colours are madder red and indigo blue shades and they often show extra weftwrapping at the joins of colour. Some have a very open feel in the design and all are subtly coloured and well balanced in their form.

Uzbek

I have previously mentioned the Uzbek handicrafts which have been made during the twentieth century and these conform to the traditions of Uzbek weaving, but in antique items vegetable dyes were almost always used and the design elements have a better balance and form. Mostly madder and indigo were used for colouring and examples include a range of red and blue tones. Kilims are mostly double interlocked but finely woven and usually utilise the large diamond motif enclosed by a narrow border of large, angular S shapes. Some gadjeri and household hangings can also be found as well as finely woven storage bags or babies' cradles. Silk is occasionally used to highlight small areas of the design.

9 Antique Village Carpets

Carpets made in a large number of villages during the nineteenth century and before, in the traditional manner and environment and using local wool, dyes and evolutionary design elements and styles, are sought after by collectors the world over and display individual characteristics which can be recognised by students of the art.

They were made in parts of what are now Turkey, Iran and the USSR and are most easily grouped into categories relating to the geographic location of production. The modern nations whose borders separate these traditional weaving centres are not relevant to the items in any way except to make it easier to group them together and for the reader to understand where it was the rugs were originally made.

The most desirable contain all vegetable dyes but I do not think that this is necessarily a prerequisite, only that rugs of this type are more valuable. Many collectors have shown interest in rugs made around the turn of the twentieth century which contain some synthetic dyes and so long as the items retain design and structural elements that make them recognisable as examples of weaving from a specific region they have some merit. The major point to stress is the value difference between a purely spontaneous product made from local materials and items which were made during the short, transitory period from a traditional setting to more commercial endeavours.

Turkey

The village rugs of Turkey offer a unique selection of individual styles, colours and designs and, although most appear in prayer rug form, they can be used in a variety of situations in the home. Traditional rugs were made as late as the 1920s and many of these show good vegetable dyes and ethnographic individuality. Early pieces, made during the sixteenth or seventeenth century, a period of Ottoman control, have been found and some of these were produced in a small workshop environment. Items made in the west of Turkey, during the nineteenth century, were produced by descendants of nomadic people who moved to the area and these are often called Bergamo rugs, after a major town. These rugs are used as a basis for design by modern rug producing groups.

Other isolated villages spontaneously produced rugs, kilims, yastik (cushion covers), grain bags, quorjin and a variety of coverlets and these smaller household items often display the finest spinning, weaving, dyeing and design techniques. Once one is familiar with a few rug types it is easy to distinguish the products of Turkey from the output of other regions.

Ghiordes

The mountains of northwest Turkey are the home of a small group of rugs named after the town of Ghiordes. Most of the carpets produced were prayer rugs and the average size was about 1.8 × 1.4 m. Some designs show a mihrab at each end of a central field containing geometric or flower motif medallion and these are often called double ended prayer rugs. The symmetrical knot was tied, to a density of about 150 per square inch, to woollen warps and wefts and the pile material was woollen, although white cotton was sometimes used to highlight areas of the design.

It is common to see a triangular, stepped mihrab, containing a hanging lantern made up of flower motifs and surrounded by multiple borders of small carnations. Colours include blue, mauve, yellow, olive green, white and a variety of red tones and pieces can be dated by the ground colour of the central compartment and the proportion of this compartment in comparison to the rest of the rug.

Ghiordes prayer rug, circa 1820, 2.0 × 1.4 m. Author's collection

One extra identifying mark in many Ghiordes rugs is what is known as a lazy line in the weaving. This can be seen on the back of the rug and looks like a line, usually diagonally placed and no more than 20 cm long, which can be seen running across the weave. This is presumably the result of an attempt, or series of attempts, to retension the pile knots and base weave and realign the weft threads.

Ghiordes carpets show a definite evolution of design formats and it is probable that they were made at a more community based level than more primitive rug types from a 'village' source, but they are rare and this listing seemed the most appropriate position for the rug type. Most examples seen date from the late eighteenth or early nineteenth century and items said to be made after the middle of the nineteenth century should not be contemplated.

Melas

Villages around Melas, in the south of Turkey, produced symmetrically knotted pile rugs with woollen base weaves which were not usually more densely knotted than 60 per square inch. Most were prayer rugs which contained a very narrow central field and small prayer arch and were surrounded by a wide border containing the crab motif. Sizes did not usually exceed 2 × 1.4 m and many small items can be found.

Students have grouped the Melas rugs into a couple of specific types, one of which is known as the Ada, or island Melas. Another major group is seen which contains a triangular mihrab and more geometric motifs and the major colours used include red, blue, mauve, white and yellow. Examples range in age from around 1840 to as late as 1920 and most of these are worthy of collection although in later pieces it is necessary to assure yourself that the dyes are of vegetable origin.

The wool used in the pile is usually very lustrous and the carpets from this centre have a loosely woven feel when they are held in the hand.

Kirsehir and Mudjur

The villages of Kirsehir and Mudjur are found in north central Turkey and the rugs from these centres are usually prayer rugs. They appear in sizes to about 1.6 × 1 m and are designed with a triangular, stepped mihrab which is surrounded by a wide border. The symmetrical knot is used to tie the woollen pile to woollen warps and wefts, which are sometimes dyed red, and the knot density is not usually greater than 100 per square inch.

Colours used include red, yellow, a range of blue tones and the occasional pink colour which can be the result of a process known as double dipping, where the same dyelot is used to dye a bright red colour then a lighter shade. There is a selection of these pieces to be found and even those produced around the turn of the twentieth century are worth

collecting as they retain the individual character of the region.

Ladik

The name Ladik refers to a group of prayer rugs which are usually long and thin in format, approximately 1.8 × 1 m, and contain tulip motifs in a compartment at the top of the mihrab. They are symmetrically knotted to a wool warp and weft and are not usually denser than 80 per square inch. The colours used include green, blue, red, mauve, yellow and white and the thin central field is usually not decorated or contains only two narrow pillars, and is surrounded by a wide border of roundish flower motifs.

Rugs of this type are sometimes called Konya/Ladik and it is presumed that there is some difficulty in assessing where they were actually made. Any Ladik prayer rug made from vegetable dyes and in traditional style before 1920 is well worth collecting and most examples seen date from the late nineteenth century.

Kirsehir prayer rug, circa 1900, 1.6 × 1.0 m. The Lindley Collection

Turkish kilim, circa 1890, 1.3 X 1.0 m. Cicim embroidery from western Turkey. The
Lindley Collection

Kilims

There are a number of groups of Turkish kilims to be seen and it is difficult in this book to go into great detail about individual design styles and techniques. All old, vegetable dyed Turkish kilims have collector appeal and there is a wide variety of design and weaving styles to be seen although the most common are slit-woven tapestry and cicim style embroidery. Often the slitweaves in a kilim have been joined by some extra weft wrapping and small S signs, said to be magic and necessary to ward off the evil eye, are embroidered, seemingly at random, onto a slit-woven kilim.

Some are made in two halves then joined together after the weaving process, others are made in one piece and are often long and thin, to 4 × 2 m. The variety of design elements is diverse and the colours used display the extreme skill of dyers from the many primitive centres of their production. It should also be noted that, as Turkish kilims have only recently (the last twenty years or so) received the focussed attention of dealers and collectors, it is possible to find items woven as late as 1930 which are worthy of collection and display the individual appeal of 'antique' carpets.

I have included two plates of kilims from different regions as a guide to styles, format and colour and once a collector has an appreciation of Turkish design motifs the kilims from this country are easily recognised, although it takes a great deal of study to begin the task of classifying examples by their specific geographic area of production.

As a guide it is common to see large central compartments containing star shaped motifs which are enclosed on either end by rows of different coloured weaving with a simple design motif, often a squared shape with three or four indentations along one end, similar in style but more coarsely drawn than the comb motif seen in Turkoman rugs. Another major group of weavings are seen with a simple central emblem of the tarantula type which is enclosed within a hooked, geometric field and surrounded by wide borders of crudely drawn, geometric style vine leaf motifs. Other kilims are more stiffly drawn and some are enclosed by a border on all sides instead of the central field being open on each side.

You will find antique Turkish kilims described in a number of ways and it is common to see a fairly broad geographical region of production in Turkish kilims as it is often difficult to discover a specific district. This should not be of concern so long as the dyes used and the feel of the motifs and design are of a recognisable age. I have noticed that many of the antique Turkish kilims I have handled have had a specific feel which is smooth but at the same time firm and gives the impression of a patina. This aspect is complementary to discussions about the quality and durability of the coarse mountain wool from which many were made. It is possible to obtain Turkish kilims from the early to mid nineteenth century and these provide exciting avenues for collection and study at relatively low cost.

The Caucasus

The Caucasus mountains were home to a diverse range of cultural and ethnic groups which existed in isolated circumstances and insulated environments until the late nineteenth century and in some cases until as late as 1910. After this time the holy Jihad of Muslims against the invading Russian armies, the genocide of Armenian people who lived not only in the Caucasus but throughout the east of Turkey and in parts of Iran (all parts of ancient Armenia) and the resultant reorganisation and collapse of traditional lifestyles caused a vast change in the weavings from the Caucasus.

Caucasian rugs offer a wide variety of weaving and design styles as well as being rare examples of a sophisticated yet primitive art which reflects a view of the world that has disappeared. Rugs from as late as the turn of the century are sold at prices which are comparable to modern, finely knotted, urban workshop rugs of the same size. The individual appeal, range of colours and designs available and the unique nature of the living environment in which they were made make Caucasian rugs one of the most desirable styles of weavings available to collectors today.

Historic rugs of the 'Dragon' or 'Sunburst' type are held in museums and large private collections and are not readily available to the general public, so I have not covered them in this book as my major aim is to provide a guide book for rugs which are available to the bulk of the population. I have concentrated on describing items made during the mid to late nineteenth century and, in some cases, to as late as the 1920s, and all of these pieces can be found on the international retail market.

Kazak

The Kazak group of rugs can be divided into a number of subgroupings which are differentiated mainly by design elements but whose weaving characteristics are also dissimilar. The Borjalu Kazak is usually symmetrically knotted to a woollen warp and weft to a density of usually no more than 50 per square inch. The knot, which keeps all the warp threads on the same level, is squarish in shape when viewed from the back and the pile is quite long, to 10 or 15 mm. Weft threads are commonly dyed a reddish brown colour and the warp ends are often braided, in the style of Kurdish rugs from the east of Turkey. The major design motifs are large hooked diamond shaped medallions which are held within a rectangular compartment and contain hooked edged triangles. Minor borders show a reciprocal diamond, geometric flower or running dog motif and the main colours used include a range of red tones, beautiful blue hues, greens, yellow and white.

Karachov Kazaks utilise a similar range of colours and include darker tones of deep royal blue and red. The wine glass and serrated leaf main border or a large squared motif are seen in combination with a reciprocal diamond pattern

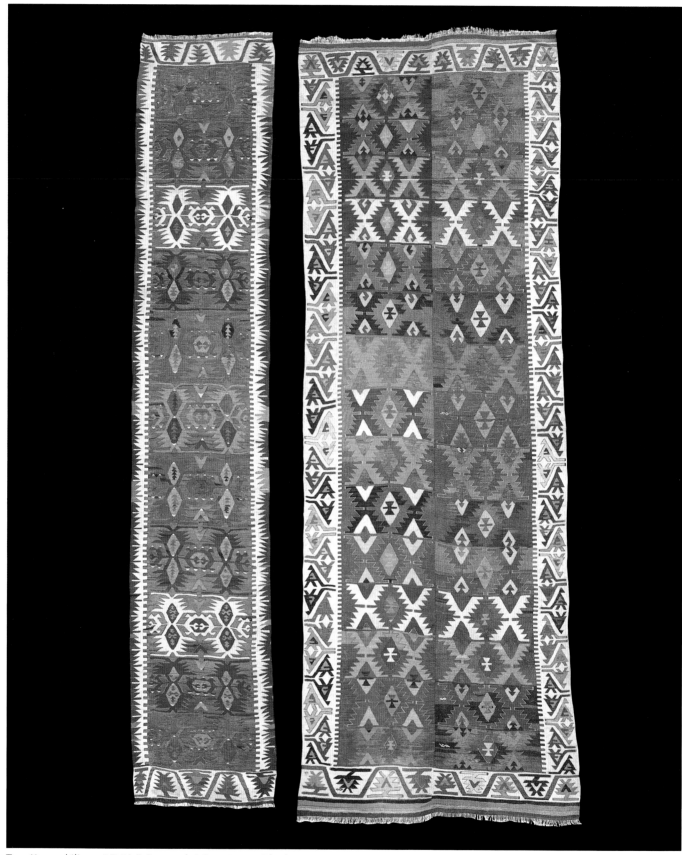

Two Konya kilims, 4.2 × 0.8 m and 4.2 × 1.4 m. The larger weaving has been woven in two narrow pieces which have been joined together. Both are from the late 19th century.
John Leach Tribal Rug and Kilim Gallery

and the major design difference is in the field where a large squared medallion or sequence of medallions appears. The symmetrical knots can be more densely packed than in Borjalu rugs and the drawing is more angular.

Frachalo pieces are usually in prayer rug form with a squared field and small, angular mihrab on one end. It is common to see an indentation in the opposing end of the field which corresponds to the mihrab. Some rugs have a more angular feel about the design or a double mihrab central field and a very triangular serrated leaf and wine glass border is common. The asymmetrical knotting of some pieces is quite dense, to 80 per square inch, but many of these were made around the turn of the century and display evidence of an organised production source.

The Sewan Kazak is commonly seen with a large medallion which has been compared to the floor layout of an Armenian church. It is very bold and rather clumsy and floats on a plain coloured ground which contains many small animal or flower motifs. The colours and border motifs used correspond to the other Kazak groups and the knotting is usually of a similar density to Frachalo pieces. All the

Shirvan pile rug, circa 1910, 2.2 × 0.9 m. Some aniline dyes and a cotton weft used in this rug. The Lindley Collection

Kazak rugs, except some Frachalo pieces, have a thick feel and most contain a beautiful, lustrous wool which is durable as well as very soft to the touch.

Shirvan

Rugs of the Shirvan group are symmetrically knotted, to a density of around 100 per square inch, on finely spun woollen warp and weft. It is common for one side of the knot to be slightly indented and in most later pieces, made between 1890 and 1920, a cotton weft and sometimes warp

Detail of Kazak pile rug from the late 19th century. The Lindley Collection

Shirvan prayer rug, 1.75 X 0.85 m. Second half of the 19th century. Nomadic Rug
Traders

can be seen as well as a mixture of chemical and vegetable dyes, including some early aniline colours which fade quite badly. Most of these pieces were made within a workshop or subcontract environment but some are worthy of collection as they display the evolution of carpet weaving in the region during the time of great cultural change.

Shirvan rugs are seen in prayer rugs which show a simple square field, covered with small diamond-enclosed geometric flowers or angular boteh motifs, and a triangular mihrab at one end. The borders often include reciprocal S shapes, small, interlinked, geometric flowers, the serrated leaf and wine glass or angular star shapes. Some of these smaller pieces, ranging in size from about 1 X 1.3 m to 1.8 X 1.2 m, show just a simple square field covered with the latticed, geometric flower motifs. They can also be found with the large Leshgi Star medallion as the major field ornament, but this is an unreliable indication of a Shirvan rug as the motif appears in many Caucasian weavings, and is common in later pieces from a wide geographical region. This may be attributed to the fact that the Leshgi tribe was in fact one of the major nomadic groups of the region and therefore came into contact with a number of isolated village groups who were exposed to this design motif. An explanation for its appearance in later pieces is probably that commercial interests were influencing design and, as this motif was better known in the market place than some others, it was perhaps easier to sell rugs with this design.

The border design known as a Kufic border is seen in rugs from the Shirvan region and can sometimes be found in combination with a plain field covered with rows of multi-coloured flowers in large runner sizes, to more than 4 X 1.2 m. Another group of weavings are seen which contain a large diamond shaped medallion on a rectangular field with triangular, double mihrab ends. These pieces are usually to about 2 X 1.2 m and display a range of colours including mauve and violet tones. Common colours found in all Shirvan rugs include a range of blue and red tones, yellow, ivory, pink and white.

Another individual type of rug which is sometimes included in the Shirvan group is known as Bidjov and shows an all over interlinked field pattern on a plain coloured ground which is enclosed by a narrow border. The field design can be in many forms although most seem to have evolved from the 'Dragon' design and include large shapes and many small motifs.

Akstafa

The most common element in rugs which are called Akstafa is a large bird-like object with long fanned tail which appears as a major design motif. It can be seen in the main field, sometimes in conjunction with large geometric medallions and often shares the plain coloured ground with a variety of smaller, primitively drawn animal, human and flower motifs. A range of rug sizes can be found and they often have a dark blue coloured ground. Prayer rugs have an

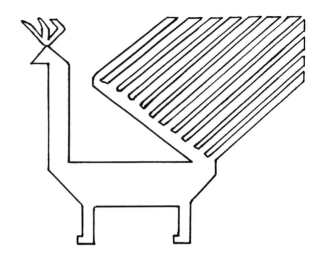

Common Akstafa design motif

angular mihrab and usually an all over latticed field decoration and the weaving style, materials and symmetrical pile knot are similar in structure to items from the Shirvan group, except that the pile is usually a little longer and the rug has a slightly stiffer feel when held in the hand. The wool used in the pile of the Akstafa rugs I have viewed felt coarse yet had a natural lustre and gave the impression of coming from a more mountain-raised sheep than many pieces from the Shirvan grouping.

Kuba

There are a number of dissimilar design elements found in Kuba rugs and it is very difficult to generalise about this aspect of the group. A more reliable method of recognising the output is to study the weave details and some of the methods of finishing which were practised. The symmetrical knots usually have a very slight indentation on one side and are not more densely packed than about 80 per square inch. They are slightly square in shape when viewed from the back of the rug and the loose warp ends are often knotted in multiple rows in a macrame style. It is more usual to see woollen weft threads than cotton and wool is nearly always used in the pile and warp materials.

Major design styles include a Kufic border, the geometric flower motif which appears in rugs from Shirvan, an all over latticed field and a group of white ground rugs with rows of abstract, geometric shapes and the Leshgi Star. Prayer rugs can be found which have an angular mihrab and are usually squarish in shape and not usually bigger than 1.7 X 1.2 m. A subgroup of small, squarish rugs which often include the Kufic or serrated leaf and wine glass borders can be found and it is usual for an all over lattice design to be used in the field of these pieces which are called *Konagend*. Another subgroup known as *Chichi* can be seen in the same range

Kuba pile rug, circa 1890, 1.45 X 1.1 m. Shows Leshgi Star medallions. The Lindley Collection

of sizes and with similar field design, but the use of a reciprocal diamond motif in the minor borders, a difference in the drawing of the geometric flower or small diamond shaped hooked motifs which cover the ground, as well as a wide main border of flower and leaf type layout, can help in differentiating between minor categories.

Daghestan

Daghestan rugs are seen in a range of sizes from about 0.9 X 1.3 m to 2.5 X 1.4 m and the occasional runner to about 3 m can be found. The style of symmetrical knotting is similar to the Shirvan group and the prayer rugs can easily be confused with those from Shirvan as they include similar lattice arrangements in the field and appear in similar size ranges. One design motif that may indicate a Daghestan rug is a large hooked diamond medallion which is repeated in a single row as the main field design. It is often combined with small animal motifs which are placed at random on the plain ground and surrounded by a main border of large angular S shapes and rows of squarish flowers. The barber

pole minor border, a thin row of alternating coloured diagonal stripes, can also be found.

The range of colours which are seen in these last three rug types includes blue tonings, from a light sky colour to rich royal blue, aqua and many bluish green tones, reds and pinks, yellow, ivory, white, apricot, black and mauve and it is possible to find a collectable piece in good condition which will suit your decorating requirements.

Kilims

The kilims from the Caucasus appear in a variety of formats including small storage bags, cradles, horse blankets and floor coverings. Weaving styles include slitwoven tapestry, weft wrapping (Soumak), extra weft brocade and mixed technique rugs. Slit-woven kilims often have large geometric motifs which are repeated in rows across the piece and most that are seen are said to be of Shirvan origin. Weft wrapped kilims appear with more sophisticated design elements and often have large medallions or a version of the Dragon design.

Iran

Azerbaijan

A range of rugs showing design elements of the Shah Sevan or Caucasian centres are usually grouped under the Azerbaijan heading. Some are quite finely woven, show a lattice type arrangement of flower vase designs in the main field and include small flower motifs in the border. The colours used range from pinks, reds, blue and dark coloured natural wool to sky blues, reds, beige tones and yellow and the symmetrical knot is usually used to tie the woollen pile to a woollen warp, although cotton may be seen in the weft threads of some examples. The weaving styles are often similar to Turkish and Iranian Kurd rugs, village weavings from neighbouring Kurdistan province of Iran and Caucasian village rugs and it must be realised that this name is often used when no other group name is deemed adequate.

Bijar

Bijar rugs were woven by Kurdish people who lived in the town of Bijar and in villages of this region of western Kurdistan. There was some commercialisation of the rug industry as Wagiri—small samplers which show design motifs and segmented medallions which were used to show buyers what designs were available in large pieces and as a pattern for weavers to work from have been found—but in many cases the weaving style and evolutionary designs were not greatly affected. Symmetrically knotted woollen pile, to a density of sometimes more than 200 per square inch, and wool warps and wefts are usual in rugs from the nineteenth century, although in some cases a cotton weft

Perepedil prayer rug, 1.6 × 1.25 m. Second half of the 19th century. Kufic border and large ram's horn type motifs are common features of this group of rugs which are named after a village near Kuba. Nomadic Rug Traders

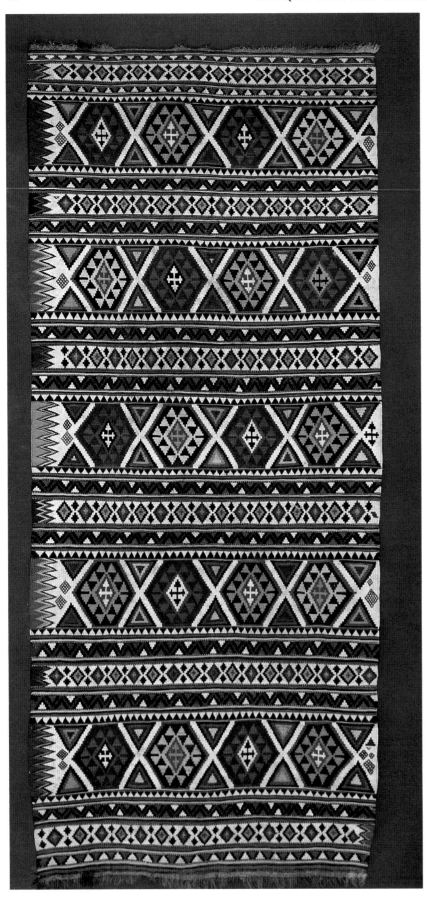

Shirvan kilim, 3.25 × 1.45 m, 19th century.
Nomadic Rug Traders

Opposite: *Azerbaijan area pile rug, circa 1890,*
1.95 × 1.05 m. The Lindley Collection

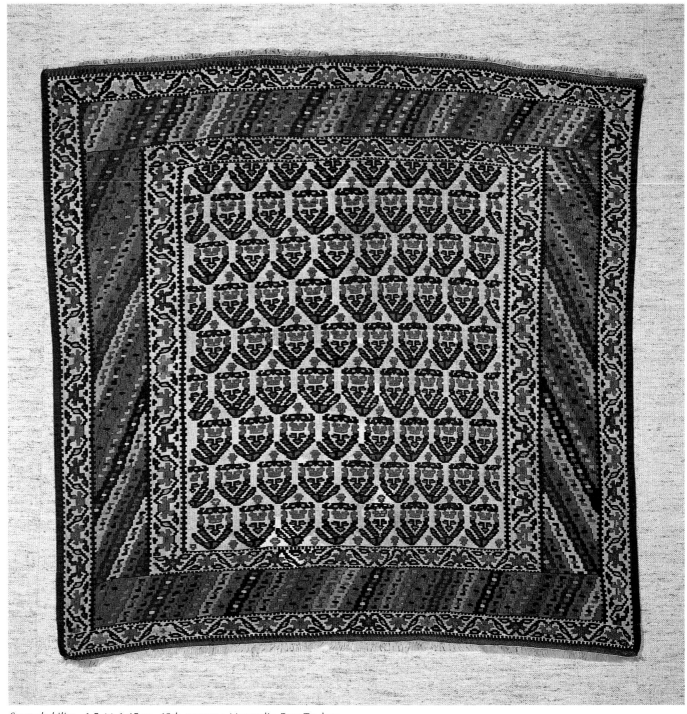

Senneh kilim, 1.5 X 1.45 m, 19th century. Nomadic Rug Traders

can be seen and after the turn of the twentieth century cotton was more often used as a base material.

A common design is a central medallion on a plain white or ivory coloured ground which shows quartered segments in each corner. Borders contain flower and vine motifs and, in some examples, the white ground can be seen at the edge of the rug and gives the impression that the ground extends beyond the border designs. In other examples, a floral, herati motif is repeated on the white or ivory ground as a background for the medallion. The main colours used include white, ivory and beige undyed wool, a range of blue and red tones, yellow, salmon pink and the occasional green.

Kilims are also woven in the region in the slitwoven tapestry technique and they are usually very finely designed with intricate flower motifs and often have an archaic feel about the drawing, with the medallions or flowers very bold in conception.

Senneh

The town of Senneh is also in Kurdistan, slightly south of Bijar, and is populated by people of Kurdish descent. The symmetrical knots are tied to cotton or sometimes woollen warps to a density of up to 180 per square inch and it is common to see cotton weft threads. The knots have a strange rasping feel when touched from the back of the rug and it seems as if the pile yarn was twisted in some way during the tying of the knot. In old pieces this is sometimes difficult to feel.

A common design shows a triangular-ended central medallion with an all over herati pattern covering the ground. In some pieces an all over boteh design covers the ground and white, ivory or dark blue are the most usual ground colours. Other colours used include a range of blue and red tones, yellow, gold, pink and tan.

The kilims from Senneh are very finely woven and usually display an all over pattern of interlinking flower motifs surrounded by narrow borders. Saddle covers, horse blankets and floor coverings can be found and the slit-woven tapestry technique was used to weave the woollen warps and wefts.

Feraghan

Feraghan rugs are usually designed with a geometric central medallion placed on a plain coloured ground or a field covered with herati motifs. The corners of the main field usually contain a complementary colour and design and the borders often utilise flower or vine and palmette motifs. The asymmetrical knot is most often used to tie the woollen pile to mostly cotton warps and wefts, although sometimes a symmetrically knotted item is found. The rugs are finely woven, from about 80 to 250 knots per square inch, and the most common colours used include brown tonings, salmon pink, a range of reds and blue hues.

Hamadan Region

The rugs of the Hamadan region of Kurdistan have been mentioned in the section on modern carpets and the traditional designs of individual towns have survived until quite recently, so I have not gone into detail about this group. Individual design elements and colours can be seen in the output from a number of towns and most of the carpets produced used a symmetrical knot and cotton warp and weft.

10 Antique Workshop Carpets

Most workshop carpets which are of interest to collectors were made in Iran during the nineteenth century and these have merit through the mixture of traditional designs and weaving styles and the input from Western market sources. Other rugs were made during this time and many are more than one hundred years old but they do not fit the requirements I have for a rug being included in this section. There are also constraints on the number of examples I can include and I hope I have selected the most desirable of the rugs which can be obtained at present.

Among early workshop rugs is a group from the west of Turkey which are often called Ushak or Bergamo and it is believed that these were produced in small workshops in the region of western Turkey which surrounds these towns at the time of the Ottoman Empire—the sixteenth and seventeenth centuries. These rugs are highly sought after and usually only available to the more wealthy collector, but I thought they should be mentioned at this point even though I have not included a full description of this type of carpet.

Heriz

The town of Heriz is situated in Azerbaijan Province, in the north-west of Iran. The small town, located in isolated hills about 100 kilometres from Tabriz, was the centre for a group of pile rugs which are symmetrically knotted, to densities of between 30 and 100 per square inch, to a cotton warp and weft. The most common design shows a squared, floral, central medallion which is quartered in each corner of the field and has a large flower attached to each end. The ground is usually a terracotta colour and white, sky blue, dark blue, salmon pink and ivory are the most common colours used. The borders usually show an angular flowerhead and leaf design and the ground colour of the main border usually corresponds to an area of colour in the medallion. A fine example appears on page 50.

Carpets from before 1850 are very valuable and the design of these early pieces is more primitive, giving the impression of more empty space in the rug as well as showing an individuality of design that is not seen in later items. The rugs from the late nineteenth century have a formal appearance and show intricate patterning and a unique balance of design that makes the Heriz group of carpets one of the most sought after among decorators and collectors. See detail photograph on page 87. When viewing examples, it is common to see some of the more coarsely woven articles referred to as Goravan, which is the name of a nearby village. Some rugs I have seen have an all over repeat pattern in the form of an angular leaf but these can be distinguished as belonging to the Heriz group through the colours, border motifs and weave type.

The name Serapi is also used in connection with the Heriz rug type and this usually relates to early carpets where similar angular medallions and a field of archaic spandrels and flowers can be seen. Most Heriz rugs are seen in large sizes from about 3 × 2 m to 4.5 × 3.5 m, although the occasional small item is seen.

Tabriz

The city of Tabriz has had a long history of carpet production and items are symmetrically knotted, to an average density of around 100 per square inch, to a cotton warp and weft. The most common design shows a large floral medallion on a plain coloured field which can contain vines, flowers and spandrels and is enclosed by a floral border. The most common sizes are large, to 4 × 3 m, although the

Detail of Heriz pile rug, 3.5 × 2.5 m. Second half of the 19th century. Robyn and Herman, Maximilian's Restaurant, Verdun, SA

occasional, very finely knotted item (to more than 300 per square inch) is seen and these usually appear in sizes of around 2 × 1.2 m. The carpets from Tabriz are among the more commercial production from Iran during the late nineteenth and early twentieth century. An example of a Tabriz carpet appears on the cover.

Mahal

A group of late nineteenth century carpets which are asymmetrically and symmetrically knotted, to densities of between 40 and 100 per square inch, on a cotton warp and weft are called Mahal. Researchers suggest that the name was a trade description for carpets made around the town of Arak, which is between Qum and Hamadan, and some are named after the designers of particular carpets. The

name Zeigler, a European designer, is often linked with Mahal rugs and his designs include medallion carpets with green and white grounds. Another common design shows an all over herati pattern in the main field and a basic flower head and vine in the border design. These pieces are usually seen with a dark blue ground colour and include pink, green, white and light blue in the design motifs.

Most Mahal carpets are seen in the large sizes, to 5 × 4 m, and they often have a blue coloured weft. The rug type is easily distinguished once a few examples have been studied and, even if no-one really knows where the name actually originated, they are accepted as an individual group of carpets.

Sarouk

Sarouk rugs are asymmetrically knotted, to a density of between 150 and 300 knots per square inch, on a cotton warp with a cotton weft that is usually dyed blue. It is common to see one side of the knot totally covered by the other and the warp threads pulled tightly atop each other, although in some pieces it is only deeply indented and causes alternate warps to be depressed. The main design usually shows a central medallion and a field of flowers and spandrels (although rugs displaying cypress and willow trees, realistic animals or tree of life type designs can also be found), and the most common colours used include dark blue and a range of red and blue tones, small quantities of olive green, ivory and white. Sizes vary from 1.2 × 0.8 m to 4 × 3 m. Some dealers and researchers have suggested that many Sarouk rugs were made in the Arak region also and that the name refers to a fine quality rug. It is suggested that both Mahal and Sarouk were originally names of rug qualities rather than types but they have come to be used to describe individual rug groups which can be recognised.

Sarouk rugs from the nineteenth century are often thought to be the finest examples of curvilinear designed workshop rugs. The drawing is elegant and the wool used was of a very good quality. The best examples also display a range of clear, vegetable dyed colours.

Kashan

The town of Kashan has a place in the history of carpets from the Persian Empire and the rugs made in the region display an individual design and weaving style. Few can be found which can be dated to before 1870 and it is believed that there was a break in carpet weaving in the region after the Persian Empire waned. The examples which can be found are asymmetrically knotted, to densities between 250 and 400 per square inch, on a cotton warp and a cotton

Opposite: *Tabriz pile rug, 3.8 X
2.8 m. Late 19th century.*
Nomadic Rug Traders

*Sarouk pile rug, 2.04 X 1.3 m.
Second half of the 19th century.*
Nomadic Rug Traders

weft, which is sometimes dyed blue. One side of the knot is usually atop the other and the warp threads are held perpendicular to each other.

The most common design shows a floral medallion with a field of flowers and spandrels and quartered medallions in each corner. The main border usually includes flower and vine motifs and there are often up to five other border stripes. Major colours seen include dark and light blue, a range of red tones and, sometimes, small amounts of green, and the most common size is about 2 X 1.4 m although larger pieces and even the occasional silk piled rug, said to be of Kashan origin, is seen.

11 Care and Maintenance of Oriental Rugs

There is much confusion about the type of maintenance oriental rugs require and many are severely damaged by neglect. Some people own very valuable pieces and believe that they must be treated with extreme care, even to the point of hanging them on a wall to avoid any wear which would result from walking on them, but forget about the damage moths can do.

Others seem to think a high monetary value means that a carpet can be treated with extreme contempt and still not suffer any permanent injury. Many people seem to disregard the rug totally when they consider the arrangement of furniture or fail to understand that carpet beetle and moths love those dark, dusty crevices in between the floor and the base of a timber chest of drawers.

A hand made carpet can last for more than a century, warming the floor for many weary feet. Furniture can be stood on top of it, but only when correct maintenance procedures are undertaken. A rug should be lifted from the floor at regular intervals and laid or hung (along the warp threads is the safest) in the sunshine. The bottom of the carpet should be inspected for signs of moths or other damage. When the rug has been thoroughly warmed on both sides by the sun it should be lightly beaten with a flat implement which contacts the surface over a wide area, or shaken to loosen the dust particles from the centre of the weave.

It can then be replaced on the floor (preferably in such a way that the major wear areas or those places which are hidden under furniture are rotated), thoroughly vacuumed, and the dining table and chairs, your bedroom furnishings or lounge suite lifted back into position atop it. The frequency of this type of cleaning schedule will vary, depending on a number of factors including the mean temperature and times of the year when the weather conditions warm up substantially, the type of destructive influence (insect, rot, etc.), the amount of wear, and the positioning and size of the carpet.

Small rugs can be given a shake prior to every vacuuming and, if they are in a situation where they receive a lot of wear, will probably not be in particular danger from moths. A wise collector will 'air' his rugs at least once a year and many who have had a sneak attack by moths in the past religiously have their carpets chemically treated by a qualified pest controller every summer.

It is wise to make contact with a pest control firm which has had experience with hand made rugs if you need chemical treatment for moth protection. Most will offer a three month warranty on moth sprays and suggest that twice yearly sprays, in the summer season, are the minimum protection against moth attack.

If a rug is dirty, it can be washed in cool water and an acceptable wool detergent. In most cases it is possible to do this at home without too much chance of damage, but there are many things to watch out for. The dyes may run, especially if the rug is kept wet for too long, the rug may twist or buckle when it is soaked in water or if it is not laid flat while drying, or some portions of the end weave or selvedges could be damaged through inexperienced handling while wet.

If you have never washed your rug before it is imperative that you consult a specialist oriental carpet cleaner or a dealer for advice on whether it is safe for you to clean it. Sometimes the dyes used in modern rugs are not water fast or there may be some other reason why it is best to have your rug professionally cleaned.

Most oriental rugs are washed when they are removed from the loom and the methods which are used are usually quite primitive but very effective. When I wash my rugs I try to imitate these traditional methods. I thoroughly wet the carpet, using a hose on the lawn or a large area of concrete. The soap is applied by hand; I use a bar soap but if a liquid is used it is best to dissolve it in some water and apply the solution directly to the pile.

When the surface of the pile has been covered with

Removing excess water from a washed carpet with the aid of a squeegee

A wet rug hanging on a wooden railing to dry

Rugs being washed in Kabul, 1971. Alan Schultz

detergent I scrub the pile with my fingers, working at any difficult stains with a soft brush. I often soak smaller pieces in a large trough or the bathtub and use a commercial wool cleaner, like you use for your best woollen jumpers. Once clean the rug is rinsed in running water. To do this with a hose requires patience and a lot of water as the stream must be applied to each side of the carpet a number of times, and the water must be brushed through the weave as well. This can be achieved by soaking the rug then leaving the hose to run underneath it at the same time as rubbing the pile, in the natural direction of the nap, with a straight edge.

After proper rinsing I squeeze the excess water from the pile with the aid of my straight edge (again pushing with the grain of the pile), let the carpet lie flat until at least half of the water has drained or evaporated, then, to speed the drying process, I hang it along the warp threads on a round, wooden railing.

Professional cleaners may use these, or a version of these methods or large specialised companies have machines which imitate these processes but speed up the drying and rinsing. The wool in some carpets has been treated in such a way that wet washing may not be desirable. There are companies which can dry wash carpets, but it is necessary to ascertain what chemicals are used as some may damage dyes or fibres.

In source countries the rugs are washed in creeks and drains and I have read that in some rug regions the carpets are laid pile down in the snow and beaten on the back so that the ingrained dust is removed at the same time as the ends of the pile are washed by the snow.

There are areas of a rug which will be worn by natural use on the floor and maintenance may be necessary to prevent further damage. Often the end weave and fringes will wear and must be consolidated by tying all the loose warp ends or chain stitching along the last exposed weft thread. The selvedges, the bindings along the edges of a rug, may also need to be replaced during the long life of a carpet.

Should damage occur to the pile, there are carpet repairers who can reknot or reweave the holes. A good repair person will be able to match the wool colours and type of weave so that the rewoven areas will be very difficult to find. A good oriental rug will last a lifetime if you care for it properly and when the value of your carpet, the pleasure it gives you and the amount of time it took to create it are considered, it is only sensible to ensure that it is adequately maintained.

12 Conclusions

I hope that after reading this book you have gained some understanding of the classification system described and the traditions involved in an oriental carpet. If you wish to know more about oriental rugs I have included a small bibliography with a list of books and catalogues which contain more information on specific rug types and recommend further study in your chosen area.

As well as book learning it is necessary to see and touch a wide variety of carpets in order to discriminate adequately between rug types and appreciate the differences between weave types and rug qualities. The only place where one can find these examples is in a retail outlet and interested persons should search their home towns for a dealer who offers a selection of rugs as well as the time, patience and knowledge which allow a potential purchaser to make discriminating choices. It will be necessary to view a number of outlets and talk with a number of dealers before a personal choice can be made regarding the one (or more) retailers who offer credible rugs at credible prices, as well as being able to enhance their collections with the necessary knowledge and appreciation of the artform.

There are many reasons why people buy an oriental carpet and some thought must be given to your personal needs and uses for such an item before any guidelines can be given on how to choose an adequate rug. The individual must assess his or her specific needs, individual tastes and reasons for purchasing a rug before the search for a reputable dealer is begun.

As a very broad guide it is probably best to stay away from anyone who regularly advertises huge discounts unless you feel very confident about your own personal knowledge of both the rugs viewed and the current, local retail price. Dealers who have a long history in the business, are involved with antique associations or specialist organisations and offer regular exhibitions of rare goods are probably the most accountable, as their products are regularly viewed by enthusiasts and collectors and are under constant scrutiny by the enlightened buying public.

Do not be afraid to ask questions about the rugs on view and be sure to make decisions which are based on your own individual needs rather than buying the items which are marketed as the best investments or the most popular product.

Be sure to remember that very few carpets offer short term speculative gains, especially if purchased at the retail level, and only buy an oriental rug if you decide the item is one you want to own and display in your home. If the rug is durable, from a traditional source, in good condition when purchased and used and maintained in the correct manner there is no doubt that you will have a long term investment in the item as it will probably last more than fifty years in a household environment.

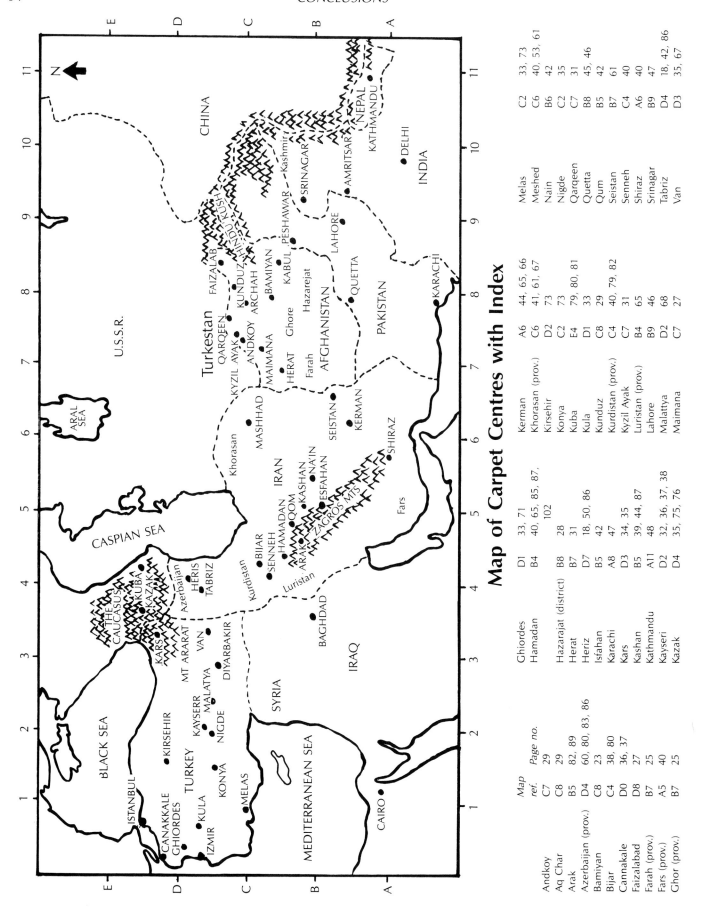

Map of Carpet Centres with Index

	Map ref.	Page no.
Andkoy	C7	29
Aq Char	C8	29
Arak	B5	82, 89
Azerbaijan (prov.)	D4	60, 80, 83, 86
Bamiyan	C8	23
Bijar	C4	38, 80
Cannakale	D0	36, 37
Faizalabad	D8	27
Farah (prov.)	B7	25
Fars (prov.)	A5	40
Ghor (prov.)	B7	25

	Map ref.	Page no.
Ghiordes	D1	33, 71
Hamadan	B4	40, 65, 85, 87, 102
Hazarajat (district)	B8	28
Herat	B7	31
Heriz	D7	18, 50, 86
Isfahan	B5	42
Karachi	A8	47
Kars	D3	34, 35
Kashan	B5	39, 44, 87
Kathmandu	A11	48
Kayseri	D2	32, 36, 37, 38
Kazak	D4	35, 75, 76

	Map ref.	Page no.
Kerman	A6	44, 65, 66
Khorasan (prov.)	C6	41, 61, 67
Kirsehir	D2	73
Konya	C2	73
Kuba	E4	79, 80, 81
Kula	D1	33
Kunduz	C8	29
Kurdistan (prov.)	C4	40, 79, 82
Kyzil Ayak	C7	31
Luristan (prov.)	B4	65
Lahore	B9	46
Malattya	D2	68
Maimana	C7	27

	Map ref.	Page no.
Melas	C2	33, 73
Meshed	C6	40, 53, 61
Nain	B6	42
Nigde	C2	35
Qarqeen	C7	31
Quetta	B8	45, 46
Qum	B5	42
Seistan	B7	61
Senneh	C4	40
Shiraz	A6	40
Srinagar	B9	47
Tabriz	D4	18, 42, 86
Van	D3	35, 67

Bibliography

It is impossible to give a full bibliography for this book as much of the information has become so much a part of my understanding of oriental carpets that I cannot remember where it was gained, but listed below are a number of books which I referred to and used to compare information when actually writing this book. They can all be used for study of specific rug types included in this book or for research into other rug groups which were omitted through lack of space and my aim to present only carpets that I have been exposed to during the last ten years and that are available on the market at present.

Tribal Rugs by Jenny Housego, Scorpion Publications, 1978.
Oriental Rugs Antique and Modern by Walter Hawley, Reprint of original book first published in 1913. Dover Publications, 1970.
Oriental Rugs Vol. 1 *Caucasian* an English translation by Ian Bennett of Doris Edder's original work. Oriental Textile Press, 1981.
Oriental Rugs Vol. 3 *The Carpets of Afghanistan* by R.D. Parsons. Oriental Textile Press, 1983.
Oriental Rug Repair by Peter Stone. Greenleaf Company, 1981.
Oriental Carpets by Ulrich Schurmann. Octopus Books, 1979.

Turkoman Tribal Rugs by Werner Loges. George Allen & Unwin, 1980.
The Arts and Crafts of Turkestan by J. Kalter. Thames & Hudson, 1984.
Textiles of Baluchistan by M. Konieczny. British Museum Publications for the Trustees of the British Museum, 1979.

Exhibition Catalogues

The Qashquai of Iran from World of Islam exhibition, Whitworth Art Gallery, Manchester, 1976.
Baluch Prayer Rugs exhibition by Adraskand Inc., California, 1982.
Kilims—The Traditional Tapestries of Turkey exhibition at The Douglas Hyde Gallery, published by Oguz Press, 1979.
Exclusively Baluch exhibition by J. Homer, Cheltenham, UK, 1986.
Discoveries from Kurdish Looms exhibition supported by Northwestern University and Mary and Leigh Block Gallery, Illinois, 1983/84.
The Rug as Art inaugural exhibition The Caspian Gallery, Sydney, 1989.
A number of auction catalogues by Phillips, London and Leeds.

I also referred to a number of editions of *Hali—The International Journal of Oriental Carpets and Textiles* dated from 1981 to 1989.

Index